Flavours of Rosello

Flavours of Rosello

Pino Iacaruso

Watercolours by Pino Iacaruso
Drawings by George Corbett DRAS. FRAS

LiveWire
Books

Copyright Pino Iacaruso 2003

All right reserved. No part of this publication may be reproduced or stored in a retrieval system or transmitted in any form or by any means, electronic, mechanical, photocopying or otherwise without the prior written permission of the publisher.

First published in 2003 by
Live Wire Books,
The Orchard,
School Lane,
Warmington,
Banbury,
OX17 1DE
Tel: 01295 690624

The right of Pino Iacaruso to be identified as the author of this work has been asserted in accordance with the Copyright, Designs and Patents Act 1988.

ISBN No. 0 9542860-2-2
A catalogue record for this book is available from the British Library.

Copies of this book can be obtained at a cost of £10.00 plus £1.50p&p from Pino Iacaruso, Rosello, Harbury
Leamington Spa, CV33 9JD. Tel: 01926 612417.

Designed by Gemini Designs

Cover design by Rosy Burke Design Associates

Back cover photograph by Caroline Iacaruso

Printed and bound in Great Britain by Dialhouse, Coventry.

DEDICATION

To my darling honey, Caroline, Edilio and Anthony

And in memory of
My mother Lina and my grandmother Concettina
Who gave me my wonderful childhood

KENSINGTON PALACE

I am delighted to give my support to Pino's recipe collection, particularly in aid of such a worthwhile cause.

Pino first came to work for us over 15 years ago. He is a superlative chef for whom pride and love are staple ingredients of all the food he prepares. We remember many special dinner parties, and have often missed his culinary skills.

We became very fond of Pino and his family and we remain good friends now he has left us and is running his own business.

I know that publishing this book has been Pino's dream for many years, and I wish him every success in this, and in whatever the future holds for him.

HRH Princess Michael of Kent

FOREWORD

By John Watkinson
Consultant ENT/Head & Neck & Thyroid Surgeon
The Cancer Centre, Queen Elizabeth Hospital,
Edgbaston, Birmingham.

I had heard of Pino Iacaruso before I met him. The famous chef had offered to give his time, free of charge, to make canapes for a Get A-Head charity function in January 1996, which David Owen had organised and which starred Rory Bremner. Coincidentally, I was then asked to see Pino who had suddenly developed a cancerous growth in his mouth. Treatment started with radiotherapy, which was followed by surgery with reconstruction that involved a graft to his face from his forearm. The rest is history.

Pino suffered his disease with great dignity and came through it a stronger man. Ably supported by his family, he returned to work and is now even more successful than before. Having sampled his wares, I pay tribute to his culinary skills and there is a saying in medicine that you should never make a patient out of a friend or a friend out of a patient. Rules are there to be broken and I value Pino not only as a patient but as a true friend and it has been a privilege to treat him.

Pino intends to donate some of the profits from this book to Get A-Head which is a charity dedicated to helping patients who have head and neck diseases, but especially those with cancer. Its aims are to contribute to research and the purchase of vital equipment as well as education and I know that Pino has benefited from its work. Get A-Head acknowledges Pino's culinary, artistic and literacy skills and,

'Remember, whatever your labours and aspirations in the noisy confusion of life, keep peace with your soul. With all its shame, drudgery and broken dreams, it is still a beautiful world.' (Desiderata, 1692).

The
Get A-Head
Charity Appeal
For Head and Neck Diseases
Including Cancer

ACKNOWLEDGEMENTS

There are many people who encouraged me to write this book. Among them I am indebted to Lynne Watkin, computer wizard, who typed the whole manuscript and helped get the recipes together, sampling along the way!

My thanks, above all, to Tim Malby who has never flagged in his enthusiasm and support for the whole project. In fact, we would not have got this far without him.

And Michael Cable and Jill Todd, our editors at Live Wire Books, who have indeed made this, my first book, possible, and who will hopefully carry on with the second book, my autobiography.

My appreciation and thanks go to George Corbett for the wonderful drawings in this book.

To Her Royal Highness, The Princess Michael of Kent, my thanks for the introduction and her continued support and friendship.

To John Watkinson, John Glaholm and Steve Dover and to so many others at The Queen Elizabeth Hospital in Birmingham I give my great affection. There are far too many to mention but special thanks go to a few in Ward E5, ENT - Caroline, Debbie, Stella, Laurey, Helen, Zoe, Lucia and Wendy. All took such great care of me and continue to do so.

And finally my darlings, Caroline and Edilio who truly make my life complete.

PINO IACARUSO

Preface

Giuseppe Iacaruso, affectionately known to everyone as Pino, cannot remember a time when he did not want to be a chef. "I was born with a wooden spoon in my mouth," he says, explaining that his father, Edilio, his uncle Luigi, and his paternal grandfather, Giuseppe, after whom he was named, were all chefs. "It's in the blood."

The Abruzzi region of Italy, where he was born and raised in the small mountain village of Rosello, is famous the world over for its chefs, most of whom started their careers in the hotels, embassies and great private houses of Rome. Young Pino was no exception, leaving home at the age of 14 to become an apprentice in the Pensione Alfa, not far from the capital's main railway station.

That was in 1963. During the next few years, with La Dolce Vita in full swing on the Via Veneto, Pino moved first to the Belgian Embassy, presided over in grand, old world aristocratic style by Ambassador Baron Poswick and renowned in diplomatic circles for the quality of the cuisine produced by head chef Eduardo Coletta. From there he went to the Hotel Michelangelo, within sight of the Vatican walls.

Next came a spell at Nyffeneger's celebrated restaurant and patisserie in Lausanne, where he perfected the art of pastry work in the Laboratoire de Patisserie before coming to England in 1970, at the invitation of Domenico Caracino, a friend and fellow chef from Rosello, to take up a position in the kitchens at the Italian Embassy.

There, in Grosvenor Square, he found himself living and working in what is regarded as one of the most beautiful houses in central London, its rooms sumptuously furnished with antiques and decorated with priceless works of art, including classic paintings from the Renaissance. It was there, also, that Pino, working under Neapolitan head chef Gino Esposito, first cooked for members of the Royal Family, as well as for Government ministers and for the many other distinguished guests who attended the glittering official functions hosted by His Excellency the Ambassador, Raimondo Manzini.

On Gino's days off, Pino would cook regular meals for the Ambassador and his mother, Signora Manzini, who lived with him in the Embassy, and they soon learned to recognise and appreciate his individual style, often making a point of passing on their compliments.

With his reputation spreading fast, Pino eventually left the Embassy for an even more prestigious position when Princess Margaret's chef, Renato Percario, also from Rosello, sought him out to become his assistant at Kensington Palace. Pino, whose bedroom in the staff quarters overlooked the Palace's private gardens, with Kensington Palace Park beyond, soon became used to the sight of the Princess and her then husband, Lord Snowdon, popping into the kitchen to see how things were going and occasionally pausing to steal a taste of whatever was simmering away on the stove. Other vivid memories from this time include the Queen coming to lunch and Princess Margaret appearing in the kitchen at Christmas time to stir the pudding, holding the wooden spoon and closing her eyes while she made a wish.

It was while he was working at Kensington Palace that Pino met his future wife, Caroline, at a champagne party held in a nearby Kensington High Street discotheque. Caroline had trained in hotel management and for many years had run the Rutland Court Hotel in Chelsea but was working by then at The Royal Academy of Dancing in Knightsbridge. When Pino explained that he was working at Kensington Palace she thought at first that he must mean the Kensington Hotel. He told Caroline that night that she was exactly the kind of girl he would like to marry and three years later, in 1975, she duly became Mrs Iacaruso.

In the meantime, Pino had left Kensington Palace to run his own kitchen in the private Chelsea home of Michael Buchanon-Michaelson, a multi-millionaire businessman and his family. A dedicated gourmet and bon viveur, his new employer would choose the menus for the day each morning over breakfast. These would always include a three-course evening meal, even on those occasions when he wasn't actually hosting a full-scale dinner party, the exquisite and carefully-chosen dishes accompanied by the finest wines from an extensive cellar to which only the butler had a key.

Following his marriage to Caroline and the arrival of their son Edilio in 1976, Pino returned to ambassadorial duties, this time at the Finnish Embassy. With Caroline also joining the staff as Major Domo, the next eight years were spent working very happily together for the Ambassador, Dr Richard Tötterman and his wife, Madame Camilla Tötterman, a charming gourmet couple who took a close personal interest in everything that was going on in the kitchen and encouraged Pino to experiment with new recipes and flavours.

At the same time, Pino also started making regular returns to Kensington Palace, having been recommended to Prince and Princess Michael of Kent by their butler, Ernest Bennett, formerly HM The Queen's First Page for over 30 years, who used to go to the Embassy from time to time to help out at dinner parties. Later, having forged a close relationship with the Kents, Pino also went to cook for them at their Gloucestershire home.

Finally leaving the Finnish Embassy after the Töttermans had ended their tour of duty, Pino went on to work at the Ivory Coast Embassy for a short period before he decided that he would like a change of pace and took a job as Senior Sous Chef at the Royal Trafalgar Thistle Hotel, where there was a fashionable brasserie. Enthusiastic about the eighties' trend towards nouvelle cuisine and delighted to be re-acquainted with the hustle, bustle and camaraderie of a constantly busy kitchen, Pino felt very much at home there until, with their son Edilio growing up, he and Caroline felt it was time to move out of London into the country.

They chose to settle in Warwickshire, not far from Caroline's family home, and there, together, they set up their own freelance catering business, Take Two Cooks and, later, As You Like It, a subsidiary specialising in wedding cakes. In the years since then, this has gone from strength to strength despite a cruel and devastating setback when Pino was diagnosed with mouth cancer in 1995 and underwent major surgery the following year.

Having thankfully survived major surgery, Pino remains as full of life and energy as ever, a wonderfully positive personality whose sublime talents as a chef are hugely in demand and who still finds time amidst an increasingly hectic work schedule to pursue his hobbies of painting and writing.

In Flavours of Rosello, his wonderfully evocative childhood recollections of a calendar year in the life of the remote village where he grew up, he has used his own words and pictures to conjure up nostalgic and mouth-watering images of a time when the simple social, economic and culinary life of a rural Italian community was still defined by the rhythms and tastes of the seasons. He has also included a wide selection of favourite recipes to satisfy appetites that will undoubtedly be whetted at the turn of every page.

As a mark of his gratitude to consultant cancer specialist Mr John Watkinson of the Queen Elizabeth Hospital, Birmingham and the team of doctors and surgeons who helped to treat him, Pino intends to donate part of the proceeds from the sale of Flavours of Rosello to the Get A-Head charity appeal for head and neck diseases, including cancer.

PROLOGUE

Prospiro Spero.
Whilst there is life there is hope.

I was raised in a small village called Rosello, in the Abruzzo region of Italy, where I was born on the 9th of June 1948 on a warm summer afternoon. My childhood days were filled with simple joys and happiness. I had loving parents, a resident grandmother and four brothers and sisters.

My memories of those years remain so clear and vivid in my mind; the haze of the summer days, the long winter months, the friendly and chatty neighbours living side by side and the laughs and tumbles of the games I used to play with my friends. We shared the same street, the same contentment and the same fun on the shiny cobbled stones of my village.

I am an Abruzzese, the Abruzzi being a mountainous region in the Appenines. At its heart, the two highest mountains are La Maiella at 8,250 feet and Il Grand Sasso at 8,850 feet. They give the bone structure and pride to the region, their distant snow-capped peaks providing the reassurance of a stable presence, like parents to their children. The Abruzzo runs down the central spine of Italy, between the Umbria region (Perugia) in the north and the Molise region in the south, bounded to the west by the Lazio region (Rome) and to the east by the Adriatic Sea. And although so far from the place where I have now made my new life, here in England, it remains very dear to my heart, the place where I still feel my roots to be.

Rosello is situated on a high plateau, 3,000 feet above sea level and is surrounded by the most beautiful mountain scenery. This is where I would go for walks with my friend, Nicolino, searching for mushrooms early in the mornings. We knew every inch of the countryside well and the exact location of the secret places where we would be most likely to find these mushrooms. Picking wild blackberries in the hedgerows was another pastime. We would gather long stems of rye grass and thread the berries onto them one by one, creating strings of blackberries like precious pearls.

At other times we would go fishing for river shrimps (*austropotamobius pallipes*) in the crytal clear waters of the nearby River Verde. We would dip our hands into the fast-running water, feeling under the stones for any sign of these amphibians with their sharp claws. They would cling around our fingers and with a quick movement we would toss them on the bank of the river. We would collect the catch and take it home for our mothers to cook in a tomato sauce, a delicious accompaniment to spaghetti.

The changing of the seasons brought different sights smells and sounds in abundance. Spring, summer, autumn and winter - each had its own unique gift to offer, and this helped to make me appreciate and respect the harmony and contrast that nature has, all of which has been a tremendous influence on my cooking and also on my painting.

My father, Edilio, went to work in Naples as a kitchen boy in restaurants and hotels, where he first learnt his skills before moving on to work in private houses. He then worked for a time at the British Embassy in Rome, eventually joining the Italian Navy as a civilian chef shortly after the war. He felt that by working for the Government, his job was assured for life, with a good salary and all the benefits that came with it, but to be away from home for long months at a time must have been an enormous sacrifice for him. He gave nearly all his working life to the Navy, staying with them for forty years until his retirement, and was awarded three medals, Gold, Silver and Bronze, by the Ministry of the Defence.

He was always a provider for his family. We never wanted for anything. Even after my brothers and sisters and I left home and went our separate ways, he continued to help us, both financially and morally. One of his great ambitions in life, which he has now fulfilled, was to build a private chapel and family burial place in the cemetery at Rosello. That is where his mother and my mother have already been laid to rest. He, meanwhile, still lives in the piazza at Rosello, now aged 79.

As a young man he was tall, slim and good-looking, always clean- shaven and well dressed. He had red hair and was nicknamed 'the Red' by everyone in the village. He rarely did any cooking when he was at home on leave, except on special occasions or when we had relatives coming. I imagine he wanted to take a break from cooking, especially as he would only be at home for a few weeks.

However, he would occasionally cure ham and make sausages to be hung up from the kitchen ceiling and smoked by the chimney fire. His biggest love apart from gardening, has always been picking mushrooms in the countryside to preserve in olive oil and store for the winter. His long absences really meant that my mother and my grandmother, who lived with us, brought up all of us five children.

I was very close to my mother, Lina Valerio. She was very sweet and kind, with gentle features, a beautiful smile, a calm reassuring manner and immense patience. She was also very tidy and organised. She used to dress well, making a lot of her own clothes on an old sewing machine she had owned ever since she was married. She would also make clothes for us children.

She had chestnut hair, brown eyes and was a little on the plump side. Her nickname was 'La Storna' after her mother and her grandmother. We were also known by the same nickname, so as to be distinguished from other people with the same Christian names. For example, I am still known as Pino, the son of Lina Della Storna. She meant the world to all of us and we still miss her terribly.

She provided us with wonderful traditional home cooking. Later, as a professional chef, whenever I tried to make Gnocchi di Patate (potato dumpling) with tomato sauce, one of our Sunday favourites, it never tasted quite the same as hers. It somehow lacked the home atmosphere, the warmth of the family and the smell of the burning log fire. It was the same with fresh tagliatelle.

My mother would start by making the dough early in in the morning, allowing it to rest for several hours before rolling it out, cutting it into long strips and cooking it. It was very hard work on the shoulders and wrists, and pasta machines being unheard of in those days. There is a kitchen utensil to make pasta alla chitarra (guitar string pasta), a classic dish of the region. It consists of a rectangular wooden frame with very fine strings, similar to a weaving loom. A rolled out sheet of dough would then be placed over it and pressed down using a rolling pin. The pasta would come out ready to cook, and looking like fine tagliatelle. Somehow, the pasta I remember from my childhood had a different texture; maybe it was the air, the local water, the flour - or possibly just my mother's magic touch.

In those days we did not have classic sauces to pour over meat dishes to make them glossy or more appetising. Neither did we spend a great deal of time attempting to decorate fish dishes with flair and imagination. The food was simple, wholesome and healthy, with fresh, good quality ingredients.

In most Italian households, life revolves around mealtimes. The tablecloth, the napkins, a basket of homemade bread and bottles of local wine were brought to the table at every meal. My family were no exception in that respect. I think I must have inherited a lot of my culinary abilities and imagination from my mother's cooking. So, really, I owe everything to her.

JANUARY

Giocattoli - tamburini, trompette, soldatini e bambole.
Toys - drums, trumpets, wooden soldiers and dolls

Snow lying deep on the ground, plumes of smoke rising straight up from the village chimney pots before gradually dispersing into the cold winter sky and the excited chatter of children echoing across the piazza - these are among my more vivid childhood recollections of a very special time of year in Rosello. January 6th - the 12th day of Christmas - is the Epiphany and, in Italy, this is when presents are traditionally given and received. Instead of Father Christmas and his sleigh, we have *La Befana*, an old lady dressed all in black, with a long skirt and a pointed witch's hat, riding around on a broomstick to deliver presents.

My friends and I, eager to show off the surprises we had found waiting for us, would gather in the piazza in the morning, making our way there along footpaths trodden down through the snow. Michel, Matteo, Nicola, Emidio, Guido and Tonio would then hang around to see what else was going on and together we would watch the passers-by. The men would either be heading towards the pub (*cantina*) for a drink and a game of cards or congregating around the fountain for a chat. The women would be going to the local grocery or paying a call on friends and neighbours to see if they needed a hand with anything.

With his loud infectious laugh, Guido was the big mischief-maker in our group and would always be the one to start the inevitable snowball fight. After the excitement and the laughter had died down we would return to our homes, our fingers numb with cold, our faces glowing.

The snow would fall heavily for days on end, covering most of the Regione Abruzzo in a thick white blanket and almost invariably leading to power cuts. It was not unusual for us to be without electricity for long periods. We always made sure that we were well stocked up with candles and, with no television to watch in those days, we would huddle around the fire to keep warm while my mother Lina Valerio, and my maternal grandmother, Concettina, would take turns to tell us old traditional village stories.

Being snow-bound was something we were used to. Either the snowplough couldn't get through or it would have broken down. Sometimes there would be just too much snow and the drivers didn't even try to clear a path through the drifts. It was the same old story every year, so we were all resigned to the situation. As long as we had enough provisions in our house we weren't too bothered. The most important necessities were warm clothing and plenty of wood to last us all through the long winter months.

As a civilian chef in the navy, my father was only at home for a few weeks every year. My grandmother, Concettina would be the first to get up in the morning, lighting the fire so that by the time we children came downstairs the kitchen would be lovely and warm. We would have hot milk and toast for breakfast before leaving for school, returning in the afternoon through the bitter cold and making straight for the fire again to thaw out.

Keeping those wood fires burning was the main concern of every household, because without them you could easily die of cold. Once a year, the town hall would provide a ton of wood per person for every household. If there were four people under one roof, four tons would be provided, if five people, five tons and so on. The smallest baby was entitled to exactly the

JANUARY

same share. But this did not come free! At end of the year you had to pay for it. And there was never enough to last the entire winter so you generally had to cut down trees from your own land or buy extra supplies from a private company.

One of my most abiding childhood memories is of the absolute silence that would descend outside on those winter nights when the skies would often be crystal clear. In the crisp, chilled air everything would be perfectly still, the whole glistening landscape transformed and illuminated by the light of a billion stars and a full silver moon that, reflected by the white snow, was bright enough to read a book by.

It was in January, at the beginning of the heavy frosts, that the pigs would be slaughtered. This was a very important ritual for the farmers, who would have been fattening their pigs all year. The process of slaughter, butchery, curing, salting and smoking would take several days, starting out in the open in front of the village farmhouses.

Early in the morning, the farmer's wife, with help from the rest of the family and their neighbours, would light a huge log fire in the kitchen fireplace, over which a large cauldron of water would be suspended from a tripod to boil.

Once the pig had been killed the boiling water would be used to scald the skin, remove the bristles and clean the skin until it was clear and white. The animal would then be suspended from an iron hook in the ceiling and weighed, before a swift, skilful cut down the length of the body allowed the removal of the intestines and other organs, after which the carcass would be left to rest and drain for a few days. The weight was very important because there would have been intense competition among the farmers to produce the heaviest pig, with much speculation, over glasses of red wine in the cantina, about who the winner would be.

The celebration feast that followed the slaughter was, of course, the best part of it all. The women wore long, flowery, decorative aprons and would be busy with large saucepans, running backwards and forwards with long wooden spoons and ladles as they set to work in the busy kitchen. Relatives, neighbours and friends were all invited to what was a bit like a banquet, with

21

FLAVOURS OF ROSELLO

everyone seated around a long table covered with the best white tablecloth.

The antipasto would be served with a mix of salami and pickled jardinière of vegetables, followed by our famous classic dish of beans and pasta soup (*pasta e fagioli*). This is delicious by itself, but can be made spicier and even tastier by adding a pinch of hot chilli powder. It was here that the adult men would start to be silly and show off, competing to see who could eat the most plates of pasta e fagioli. Francesco Cimino, my godfather's father, was a big, tall man, renowed throughout the village in his younger days for his ability to get through up to eight platefuls before tucking into grilled pork chops (*costolette di maiale alla grilla*) with fried potatoes and vegetables, fruit and cheese and plenty to drink. I don't think anybody ever managed to beat his record.

Once the carcass had been hung sufficiently, maestro Mercurio La Penna the village's resident freelance master butcher, would be called in to butcher it. The legs and shoulder would be made into prosciutto, a type of parma ham cured with a lot of sea salt. This would be left in a wooden box in a cool place for thirty days so that the salt slowly penetrated the meat. It would then be rinsed under cold water, dried with a cloth and sprinkled with very hot chillies on the exposed bone to further preserve it.

Sausage meat would be preserved in terracotta jars with pork fat while fine salamis would be hung up on long wooden sticks running between hooks in the ceiling near the chimney, to be dried and smoked by the kitchen fire. The kitchen would end up looking like a delicatessen shop. No part of the animal was ever wasted or thrown away, every last bit being carefully stored or preserved in some way, to be eaten throughout the rest of the year.

Homemade bread (*Il pane*) was always in plentiful supply, an essential part of our diet. Fermenting yeast would be borrowed from whichever neighbour had last been using it. One of us children would be sent round to our Aunties Ornina, Lucia or Vicenza to fetch it and then return it later when we had finished with it. The yeast was kept in an old terracotta bowl. The glaze was cracked and the rim very badly chipped and yet I remember that we were frightened of dropping it on the floor and breaking it. It had been around so

JANUARY

long that it was like some priceless antique. That poor terracotta bowl must have been touched by hundreds of people and was familiar with every household in the neighbourhood as everyone used the yeast.

My grandmother was the expert in our family when it came to baking bread. This was a duty she carried out every other week, always following the same, careful ritual. As evening approached, she would first change her dress, then put on a white apron and tie a large handkerchief around her head to stop her hair from getting in the way. In one corner of the kitchen we had a large wooden chest that stood about waist high, with a sliding lid that you could pull off by sliding it towards you. She would take this lid, turn it upside down and place it over the kitchen table to use as a convenient worktop on which to roll out the dough and let it rise.

She would start by weighing out the flour with an old brass hand scale adding a few pinches of grain salt, the yeast and just the right amount of water. The dough was then mixed and kneaded with her strong, experienced hands until the exact consistency was reached. After that she would pause to get her breath back. Then, making the sign of the cross on the dough with a sharp knife and saying a few words in dialect to bless it - and to ensure that it would rise well - she would cover it with a thick white cloth and leave it to rise overnight.

At the crack of dawn the next morning, she would be up kneading and punching the dough once again. Exactly the right amount for each loaf would then be weighed out, rolled into a round shape and placed on the well-floured worktop to prove.

Like most people in the village, we didn't have our own oven at home. There just wasn't room in our tiny kitchen. Instead, we used the communal bakery where the owner, Inessa, ran her own little business. You could buy a huge crusty loaf from her or you could pay a small amount to use her oven to bake your own. She would tell you in advance when it would be available. My grandmother would roll a kitchen towel into a large round sausage, place it on her head and balance the lid with the proven dough on top of that. She would then walk quickly down the steep and cobbled streets to the bakery, with me and my brothers and sisters following behind her in a procession. As soon as you walked into the bakery you could feel the heat of the oven and smell the wonderful aroma of the freshly baked bread. Big sacks of flour would be piled one on top of the other, with stacks of chopped wood at the side of the oven for the fire. There would also be a bucket of cold water and a mop. This was used to cool down the hot oven base before each batch of baking.

Sometimes, as a special treat for us children, my grandmother would make the rustic pizza bread, *Pan di Focaccia*. This was not like it is today, with tomato sauce and all its trimmings. Instead, the simple dough was flattened and rounded, and a good strong olive oil was poured over it. It was then sprinkled with oregano, and dusted with a few grains of crushed rock salt. There might also be one or two fillets of anchovy and maybe some thinly sliced red onions, tomatoes, black olives and a few sweet basil leaves to give extra flavour. It would then be left to rise before being baked until it was a crusty brown at the edges and hollow and flat in the middle. Before it had cooled it would be cut into wedges, filled with homemade salami, mortadella or cheese and eaten straightaway. It was so delicious - all these years later I can close my eyes and still vividly recall the taste.

JANUARY

PASTA E FAGIOLI
BEANS AND PASTA SOUP

1 small onion finely chopped
2 tbsp olive oil
125g / 4 oz bacon cut up in small strips (optional)
1 clove of garlic crushed
400g / 14 oz tinned Italian tomatoes, cut up with their juice
2 tbsp chopped fresh parsley
400g / 14 oz cannellini beans
$^1/_2$ litre / 1 pint from the cooked beans water (if using dried beans)
1 litre / 2 pints pasta stock
200g / 7 oz macaroni or spaghetti broken into 2cm/1 in long
Salt and fresh ground black pepper
(hot chilli powder optional)

Put the onion in a fairly large saucepan, with the oil and fry over a moderate heat until transparent. Add the bacon and the garlic and cook for 6 to 8 minutes stirring all the time. Add the tomatoes and their juices, parsley and season with little salt and pepper and cook for 10 minutes on medium heat. Then add the drained beans and the bean water. If using tinned beans, drain from tin and add 1 pint fresh water. Stir thoroughly. Let the beans cook in the tomato sauce to combine the flavours for about 10 minutes. Meanwhile cook the pasta in salted water in a separate saucepan.

Before draining, reserve about 1 litre / 2 pints of pasta water. Drain the pasta when it is very firm to the bite (al dente), add to the beans and tomatoes to the saucepan, stir and check the soup for thickness. Add more pasta water if needed. This soup should be runny. Adjust seasoning.

Serves: 6 or more
Preparation: 30 minutes
Cooking: 40 minutes

POMODORI RIPIENE
STUFFED TOMATOES

12 small tomatoes
30g / 1 oż butter
4 tbsp olive oil
1 large spring onion or shallot, chopped
2 small cloves of garlic, crushed
1 tbsp finely chopped parsley, or fresh sweet basil
100g / 4 oz fresh breadcrumbs
Salt and freshly ground black pepper

Choose small tomatoes that are ripe but firm. Cut the tops off and put to one side. Gently remove the flesh with a melon baller or small teaspoon to retain the shape of the tomatoes. Chop the flesh roughly and put to one side.

In a frying pan melt the butter and the oil, add the onion and fry gently to soften. Stir in the garlic, but do not let it burn. Add the tomato flesh, chopped parsley and seasoning. Mix well and cook for 2 - 3 minutes. Stir in the breadcrumbs and remove from the heat. Adjust seasoning.

Fill the tomatoes with the help of a teaspoon, replace the tops and bake in an earthenware dish with a few drops of olive oil.

Chef's note: This is a good and tasty vegetable accompaniment that is always in season and will brighten up any dish.

Serves: 6
Preparation: 15 minutes
Cooking: 20 minutes
Oven: 180°C/350°F/Gas 4

JANUARY

PANE DI ROSELLO
BREAD - ROSELLO STYLE

500g / 1 lb 2 oz strong plain flour
$^{1}/_{2}$ tsp of salt
30g / 1 oz fresh yeast
1 tbsp olive oil
300ml / $^{1}/_{2}$ pint tepid water

Sieve together the flour and salt. Dissolve the yeast in the tepid water, add the olive oil and mix into the dry ingredients. If necessary, add a little more water to make a soft (but not too sticky) dough. Transfer the dough to a clean work surface and knead it. It can take up to 10 minutes to become really smooth. You need to be gentle but firm. Place the ball of dough in front of you and keep rotating. When the dough is smooth and springy, put it into a clean bowl dusted with flour. Use a sharp knife to make a cross on the top, cover with a cloth and leave to rise until almost double in size in a warm place, away from draughts. This process can take anything from 45 minutes to $1^{1}/_{2}$ hours.

When the dough has fully risen, put it back on the work surface and knead, this time to push out the bubbles of carbon dioxide created by the yeast. Knead until the dough is back to its original size and feels firm. Shape the dough into a ball then place it on a lightly oiled and floured baking tray. Brush the top of the dough with a little salted water and cover loosely with cling film. Leave in the same warm, draught-free place to rise again to almost double in size. Put the loaf into the oven and bake until crusty on the outside and the base sounds hollow when tapped. Place on a wire rack to cool.

Preparation: 20 minutes
Rising Process: 1 hour
Cooking: 30 minutes
Oven: 220°C/425°F/Gas 7

FLAVOURS OF ROSELLO

LEGUMI DI CAMPAGNA
COUNTRY VEGETABLES

This is a very attractive and unusual way of serving these vegetables. This dish can be made in advance and reheated before serving.

1 small green savoy cabbage
1 medium swede
2 medium parsnips, cored
4 medium carrots
2 tender leeks, trimmed
Salt
Freshly ground black pepper
A few fresh chives

Peel 6 good leaves from the cabbage and rinse them well. Cut each leaf in half, remove the stalk, blanch for 3-4 minutes, cool and set aside as these will be used to wrap around the other vegetables.
Peel the swede, parsnips and carrots. Cut them into 6 cm / $2^{1}/_{2}$ inch sticks long of no more than 1cm / $^{1}/_{2}$ inch width. Cook in boiling water for a few minutes, but still firm. Drain, cool under cold water and set aside.

Cut the leeks in half lengthwise, remove any outer leaves, wash well and blanch for 1-2 minutes. Drain, cool. Cut the leeks to the same length as the other vegetables and add to the other vegetables. Put the chives in a bowl and pour boiling water over them to soften them. The chives will be used to tie the cabbage parcels together.

Place the vegetables on a board and season lightly. Divide into 12 equal portions and wrap each portion of vegetables with half a cabbage leaf. Tie the cabbage leaf with some chives to hold the parcel together. Trim the cabbage leaves so that the vegetables sticks inside the parcels can be seen.

JANUARY

Put the parcels into an ovenproof dish, add a little seasoning, and then add 2 knobs of butter and 6 tablespoons of water. Cover with foil or a lid and reheat in the oven. Serve hot.

Serves: 6
Preparation: 30 minutes
Cooking: 20 minutes
Oven: 170C/325°F/Gas 3

FLAVOURS OF ROSELLO

ANTIPASTO CON SALAMI
HORS-D'OEUVRE

1 jar of pickled jardiniere of vegetables
6 slices of Parma ham
6 slices of salami Milano
6 slices of Bresaola
12 green olives and 12 black olives
6 small artichokes in oil, drained
12 sun-dried tomatoes in oil, drained
12 basil leaves to decorate

Drain the pickled vegetables. Divide the ingredients onto six plates. Before serving, put a little swirl of olive oil on the meat and a few rounds of black pepper on the Parma ham. Serve with warmed Italian bread.

Serves: 6
Preparation: 20 minutes.

JANUARY

COSTOLETTE DI MAIALE ALLA GRIGLIA
GRILLED PORK CHOPS WITH GHERKINS

You can serve these pork chops with a cream and gherkins sauce. The combination goes well together.

6 pork rib chops weighing about 180g / 6 oz each
300ml / 9 fl oz double cream
6 gherkins sliced
6 gherkins cut into small strips to decorate
1 medium onion, finely chopped
2 tsp English mustard
A little oil
60g / 2 oz of butter
Salt. Freshly ground black pepper.

Mix the cream, gherkins and mustard in a bowl. Leave to marinate for 10 minutes. Place the meat into a dish and coat with a little oil on both sides. Cook the pork chops on a hot griddle or on a barbeque and cook for 4 minutes on each side. Season and transfer to a dish and keep warm.

To make the sauce: In a frying pan, heat the butter, add the onions and sweat for about 5 minutes on a low heat until transparent.

Add the cream mixture, bring to the boil and allow to thicken for 2 - 3 minutes or until it will coat the back of a wooden spoon. Adjust the seasoning, strain into a bowl.

To assemble the dish: Place the pork chops on individual plates or on a large serving dish. Pour over the sauce and garnish with the gherkin strips.

Serves: 6
Preparation: 20 minutes
Cooking time: 15 minutes

FLAVOURS OF ROSELLO

TIRAMISU

This is my own version on the traditional way of making Tiramisu. It gives it a touch of class, making it especially suitable for a dinner party.

1 packet sponge fingers
250g / 8 oz Marscarpone cheese (or cream cheese if you prefer)
3 eggs, size 4, separated
125g / 4 oz icing sugar
Pinch of salt
2 tbsp cocoa powder

Rum syrup:
6 tbsp caster sugar
12 tbsp boiling water
4 tbsp rum
4 tbsp fresh strong coffee

Prepare the rum syrup. Beat the egg yolks with half the icing sugar. In a bowl, soften and smooth the cheese with a wooden spoon. Mix with the egg yolks. Beat the egg whites until they are light and have doubled in volume. Add remaining icing sugar a little at a time. Continue to beat until the whites are shiny and form peaks. Gently fold into the cheese mixture.

Place 8-9 sponge fingers into the bowl, soak with a few tablespoons of rum syrup and pour half the cheese mixture over it. Dip 8-9 sponge fingers into rum syrup in another bowl and then lay them over the cheese mixture. Pour the remaining mixture on top. Refrigerate for several hours to set or leave overnight. Before serving, dust with cocoa powder. Serve in a large glass bowl or 6 tall glasses.

Serves: 6 or more
Preparation: 20 minutes

FEBRUARY

Il mese degli scherzi e delle mashere
The month of masks and fun

February was still a wintry month and the smell of woodsmoke would be strong in the crisp, cold air. By now the snow would have been on the ground for over four months, but still it was not unusual to find that more was on its way. Sometimes the drifts would be more than two metres high, making it difficult to get out of the house. Only the adults would venture outside, my mother and grandmother to fetch more logs from our cellar and farmers to feed their animals.

After the snow had settled that high, it could become very dangerous once the sun came out again and it started to melt. This would make it very heavy. Concerned for people's safety, the mayor, Domenico Cimino, would then send out Giovanni, the town crier *(Il banditore)*, to warn everybody. Equipped with an old brass trumpet, Giovanni would blow it loudly a couple of times and then shout at the top of his voice: "Every householder has to remove the snow from their rooftops in case they cave in." The Town Hall *(Il Municipio)*

FLAVOURS OF ROSELLO

could not provide any alternative accommodation so everybody always obeyed that order straightaway!

From our kitchen window I could see people walking on the slippery footpath in the street outside. The women would cover their heads with thick woollen shawls, pulling them tight with one hand to cover the mouth and nose, leaving only the eyes exposed to the biting wind. The men wrapped themselves in long, heavy overcoats, leather boots and woollen gloves. Nobody wanted to catch a cold or influenza.

Looking towards the open countryside, the white blanket of snow would extend as far as my eyes could see, a vast landscape in which the houses gave way to hills, trees and mountains. It looked bleak and cold at this time of year and yet still it was beautiful. Nearby, our village pine forest, thick with tall trees and long, heavy branches weighed down by the snow, took on a ghostly appearance. I can't ever remember making a snowman as a youngster. When you live in a place where it snows for four or five months at a time you are always planning to make one the next year but never quite getting round to it.

I remember standing in the piazza one lunchtime, looking around to see who was out and about and then deciding to go and visit a friend, Ennio, who lived with his parents, Antonio and Lucia. They rented a small first floor apartment at the Palazzo. The door to the apartment opened straight into a kitchen where the family ate. Antonio was sitting next to the roaring fire, his legs stretched out, smoking a pipe with a contented look on his face. Clearly, he had just finished a good lunch. Lucia was clearing the table and told me to sit down. "Would you like something to eat?" she asked. "We had fox stew today. Antonio shot it a few days ago and I cooked it with a smile and a pinch of pleasure."

A plate was put in front of me with the stew, mashed potato, vegetables and a glass of wine. Antonio, Lucia and Ennio were watching closely to see what I thought of it and how I reacted to the first mouthful. In fact, it wasn't too bad, surprisingly tender dark meat with an earthy, gamey sort of taste and I soon cleared my plate. This was the first and only occasion on which I have

34

FEBRUARY

ever tried fox, but I am sure that they must have eaten it many times. I have included a recipe for those who might want to contest at least one half of Oscar Wilde's assertion about "the unspeakable in full pursuit of the uneatable"!

February is the month of fun and masks and, as youngsters, my friends and I would start to get very excited as the days passed and the time of the Carnival approached. We would spend hours planning how to dress up in impressive costumes borrowed from mothers and sisters. We would wear masks bought from the village shop or simply paint our faces with coal dust before going from door-to-door, asking to be allowed in. "Ce permesso la maskera?" we would ask. It was a time for jokes and people were not supposed to get too upset if they were teased a bit. There were always some who would shout at us through the door to go away, but most people liked the tradition and fun of the Carnival and would invite us in. Once inside, we would perform a little song and dance, hoping to be given sweets and chocolate or even, if we were very lucky, sausages.

The first big holiday of the year comes in February, with the week of Mardi Gras. The day before Ash Wednesday (*Mercoledi delle Ceneri*) is eagerly awaited throughout Italy, as every town and village prepares to celebrate Carnival, each in its own different way, with events reflecting local historical connections and traditions. Some of the larger ones are very well known, attracting visitors from all over the world. The oldest and most famous of all is probably that of Venice, during which the whole city comes alive with masked and costumed revellers, parading and marching through the maze of narrow streets and squares. Those of Viareggio in Tuscany and Ivrea in Piedmont are also especially renowned.

The festivities can last up to four days, with spectacular processions, gigantic floats and models of public figures made from papier-mâché. We learned about these traditional celebrations at school, where our teachers would tell us all about the famous Italian masks inspired by the medieval Commedia dell'Arte, the improvisational comedy theatre company, and such stock characters such as Arlecchino from Bergamo, Pulcinella from the

FLAVOURS OF ROSELLO

Theatre of Naples and Gianduia from Turin, with his famous comic marionette. The most famous of these characters was Harlequin, with his diamond shaped multicoloured costume. Harlequin was a zanni, a comic character, both as thick as a post and sly as a fox and who specialised in all sorts of acrobatic tricks. Together with Pulcinella, he was a fore-runner of the Punch and Judy shows.

In our little village, we didn't have all these fancy costumes and floats, but celebrated in our own quiet and simple way. The highpoint came on the last day with Mardi Gras itself, a grand get-together for family and friends. A traditional meal would be served, usually consisting of home-made potato dumplings (*gnocchi di patate*) or polenta, made with cornflour and roast sausages, and a main course of pork fillet with gherkins and cream (*filetto di maiale con citrioli e panna*).

To finish the meal, my grandmother would make little sweet fritters (*tercinelle*). These are delicious little pastries cut to finger size, deep fried in hot oil and rolled in caster sugar. She used to spoil us with these treats and both adults and children alike could be very greedy! This, however, was our last indulgence before the restrictions of Lent. The next six weeks were traditionally a time of fasting (*giorni magri*), when the church forbade the eating of meat and old Don Peppe, our village priest, encouraged strict observance.

Very popular with the adults at this time, especially my grandmother, was a bread dish called pancotto. This consisted of fresh, thinly-sliced home-made bread, layered in an oven-proof dish, moistened with a swirl of olive oil, and then baked in tomato sauce with thinly sliced onions and finely-chopped garlic. I think of this as a savoury variation of the classic bread and butter pudding, one of my favourite English puddings.

FEBRUARY

SEDANO E UOVA AFFOCATE GRATINATE
CELERIAC AND POACHED EGGS AU GRATIN

This is one of Princess Michael of Kent's favourite dishes, she often requested it for a dinner party.

700g / 1 ¹/₂lb celeriac, cleaned, peeled and diced
1 tbsp lemon juice
Salt and freshly ground black pepper
500g / 1 lb 2 oz peeled potatoes, sliced
100ml / 3 fl oz boiled whipping cream
Butter (walnut sized piece)
6 eggs, size 1 poached
125g / 4 oz Gruyere or Cheddar cheese, grated
1 tbsp chopped parsley
1 tbsp breadcrumbs

Boil the celeriac in plenty of water with salt and lemon juice until soft. Boil the potatoes until cooked. Add the celeriac to the potatoes and mash well together or put through a vegetable mill. Add the butter and boiled cream and beat with a wooden spoon until fluffy. Add seasoning.

Put the mixture into an ovenproof dish. Smooth the top and keep warm.

Lightly poach the eggs in boiling water with salt and a few drops of vinegar for 2 minutes. Lift them out of the pan and trim off some of the solid white. Place the eggs on top of the celeriac and potato purée. Mix the cheese with the parsley and breadcrumbs and sprinkle over the eggs. Place under a very hot grill until the cheese is brown and serve.

This dish makes a very good starter. It is light, tasty, easy to make, and goes well as a vegetarian dish.

Serves: 6
Preparation: 20 minutes
Cooking: 30 minutes

FLAVOURS OF ROSELLO

VOLPE IN MARINATA
MARINATED FOX

I always felt sure I could re-create Lucia's fox dish making it more palatable as well as acceptable - after all we eat rabbit, hare and venison. Obtaining the fox is another matter! Perhaps a gamekeeper may oblige.

1 fox dressed and prepared for the marinade.

Marinade
1 bottle strong red wine
2 bay leaves
2 shallots chopped
2 garlic cloves
2 tbsp tomato puree
2 tbsp olive oil
10 juniper berries

Ingredients:
60 m / ¹/₂ fl oz olive oil
30g / 1oz flour
6 tbsp brandy poured into a glass
salt and freshly ground black pepper
2 sprigs of thyme and parsley

Garnish:
200g / 7 oz back bacon chopped and boiled
200 / 7 oz button mushrooms
20 small shallots
100 ml / 3fl.oz double cream

Cut the fox into pieces and leave under running cold water for at least one

FEBRUARY

hour to clean and get rid of the clay smell. Drain.

In a large bowl, mix the wine, bay leaves, shallots, garlic, tomato puree, olive oil and the juniper berries. Add the meat and cover with cling film and leave overnight in the fridge.

Remove the meat with a slotted spoon and drain well in a colander over the bowl containing the marinade. Pat dry with kitchen paper and coat the pieces with the flour. Heat the oil in a fairly large saucepan and brown the meat on all sides over a lively heat. Pour in the brandy and set alight to flambé.

Season with salt and pepper. Add all the marinade, the stock and the herbs. Cover and place the saucepan in the preheated oven to cook.

Meanwhile fry the bacon with a little oil in a frying pan until crisp. Remove and set aside. Add the mushrooms cut in halves and cook on a lively heat until lightly brown. Add a little seasoning and mix with the bacon.

In a small pan put the shallots with 5 tablespoons of water, 2 tablespoons of melted butter, 2 good pinches of caster sugar, a pinch of salt and a few rounds of pepper. Cover and cook on a low heat for 15 minutes. Remove the lid and allow the shallots to caramelise. Add to the bacon and mushrooms.

Towards the last half hour of cooking, mix the other ingredients into the stew. Return to the oven to finish off the cooking and check whether the meat is properly cooked.

Lift the meat and the garnish out of the pan onto a dish and leave to stand in a warm place. Strain the liquid into a clean saucepan. Push all the vegetables through a fine sieve and add to the liquid.

Thicken the sauce lightly with a little cornflour mixed in water and adjust the seasoning.

Serve with buttered tagliatelle and Parmesan cheese.

Serves: 6 or more
Preparation: 1 hour
Cooking time: 2 hours
Oven: 180 C/375 F/Gas 5

FLAVOURS OF ROSELLO

GNOCCHI DI PATATE
POTATO DUMPLING

This was our Sunday lunch treat, and one of our favourite dishes of all time. I remember our mother making the gnocchi, as it was a good and tasty meal with which to spoil us.

700g / 1 lb boiling potatoes (preferably King Edward)
200g / 7 oz good plain flour
1 egg, lightly beaten
$\frac{1}{2}$ tsp salt

Tomato sauce: (see page 42)

To serve:
4-5 tablespoons freshly grated
Parmesan cheese
Freshly ground black pepper

Boil the potatoes in their skins, peel, and then put through a vegetable mill directly on to a floured surface. Do not flatten them, as they should retain some fluffiness. Allow cooling, and then make a well in the middle. Drop in the egg and sift the flour into the mixture with the salt. Now gently bring everything together with your hands and knead to a dryish consistency. At this stage, you may need a little more flour, both on the surface and in the mixture. The ideal consistency should be similar to a soft pastry.

Now cut the dough into 3-4 pieces and roll the dough into long sausage shapes about 2cm/ 3/4 inch in diameter, then cut into bite size pieces. Dust lightly with flour and put on a tray over a towel. Leave in a cool place to rest for 30 minutes and begin to shape them. Take a fork and, holding it in the left hand, prongs pointing uppermost, pick up one gnocchi, with your

FEBRUARY

thumb, push the gnocchi down the prongs to make a ridged impression and, at the same time, form a depression on the other side with your thumb. This is the desired shape so that they hold any sauce that you want to use. Once all the gnocchi are formed, place them on the floured tray.

Set a large pan of salted water to boil and drop the gnocchi in to cook. Simmer until they float to the surface, and then give them a further 20-30 seconds. Lift out with a slotted spoon, drain well and place in a heated dish. Pour over the tomato sauce and sprinkle Parmesan cheese all over. Grind over plenty of black pepper. Serve immediately.

Serves: 6 or more
Preparation: 45 minutes
Cooking: 15-20 minutes.

FLAVOURS OF ROSELLO

SALSA AL POMODORO
TOMATO SAUCE

800g / 1lb 12 oz Italian plum peeled tomatoes
6 tbsp olive oil
1 small onion, finely chopped
1 clove of garlic, crushed
1 tbsp tomato purée
1 good pinch each of fresh parsley, thyme and marjoram
10 leaves of sweet basil
1 good pinch sugar
Salt and freshly ground black pepper

  Pour the oil into a saucepan; add the onion and garlic and fry over a low heat until the onion is soft but not brown. Add the tomato juice and chop the canned tomatoes to a pulp with a knife, before adding them to the pan, then add the tomato purée and the mixed herbs.

  Bring to the boil, then simmer, and stirring occasionally to prevent sticking. Add the sweet basil at the end of cooking. Adjust seasoning and the sauce is ready to serve.

Chef's note: I like to make it with baby cherry tomatoes. It really captures the taste of the fresh fruit. Simply substitute the peeled tomatoes. Cook in a fairly large frying pan so as not to squash them. And follow the recipe as above. Delicious!

Makes: 600g / 1 lb. 5 oz
Preparation: 10 minutes
Cooking: 20 minutes

FEBRUARY

POLENTA CON SALSICCIA
POLENTA WITH SAUSAGES

During the cold winter months the polenta became a rite. But we soon grew very tired of having it over and over again. Returning from school we would ask our mother: "What are we having for lunch today?" And she would reply: "Polenta today." "Not again!" we moaned. To which mother would say: "It's only for today, tomorrow I will cook something different."

1.1 litres / 2 pints water
1 tbsp salt
250g / 8oz course grained yellow cornmeal
Freshly grated Parmesan cheese to sprinkle on top
Tomato sauce: (see page 42)
700g / 1 ½ lb good pork sausages

Make the tomato sauce, grill the sausages, cut into bite size pieces and put in the sauce. Keep warm.

Bring the water to the boil in a large, heavy saucepan. Add salt and, keeping the water boiling, add the cornmeal in a very thin stream, letting a fistful run through nearly closed fingers. Ensure that the water is kept on a slow boil and that you stir constantly with a balloon whisk.

Once all the cornmeal is added begin to stir with a wooden spoon, bringing the mixture up from the bottom of the pan and loosening it from the sides - the cornmeal becomes "*polenta*" when it forms a mass that pulls cleanly from the sides of the pan.

When done, pour the polenta into an earthenware dish and pour the tomato and sausage sauce over. Serve piping hot.

Chef's note: This is a second course, it takes the place of pasta or rice.

Serves: 6
Cooking time: 15-20 minutes

FLAVOURS OF ROSELLO

TERCINELLE
SWEET FRITTERS

My sister Giovanna gave this recipe to me. It is a dish that she makes to this day from the recipe handed down by our mother and grandmother. She varies it by adding 100g / 4 oz of potato purée for extra lightness and texture.

500g / 1 lb 2 oz plain flour
1 egg, size 4
2 tbsp caster sugar
15g / ¹/₂ oz fresh yeast
100ml / 3 fl oz warm milk
1 tbsp olive oil
A few drops vanilla essence
750ml / 1¹/₂ pints cooking oil

In a small bowl, put the flour, the lightly beaten egg, the sugar and the vanilla. Bring the milk to boil and leave to cool. Add the yeast and the olive oil to the milk and stir. Pour in the flour-egg mixture and work in by hand. Turn the dough out on your worktop and roll into a ball. Return the dough to a bowl, make a cross in the dough, and cover the bowl with a tea towel and leave to prove in a warm place. Knead the dough and roll it into a two-inch sausage shape.

Meanwhile heat the oil in a shallow pan. Cut discs ¹/₂cm / ¹/₄ in thick and cut in half again into semicircle shapes. Quickly shape the semi-circle to end up with a mini baton. Dip the baton into warm oil and quickly fry till a light gold colour. Roll in caster sugar, lift onto kitchen paper and they are then ready to eat.

Makes about: 70
Preparation: 20 minutes
Proving time: 1 hour 15 minutes

MARCH

I santi in paradiso non mangiano che linguini al pomodoro
The saints in paradise eat nothing but linguini al pomodoro

After the long winter months came the first warm, bright sunny days of spring that we had all been longing for. Melting snow from the surrounding mountains and hilltops ran down into the valleys. At this time the landscape was still sleeping, but, gradually, the woods and fields would become greener, then highlighted with the blossom of fruit trees. Newborn lambs would appear in the meadows and to see them gambolling and jumping in the air, so full of life, created a beautiful, joyful atmosphere and raised the spirits. This is still very much associated in my mind with the month of March.

March 19th, is San Giuseppe Day (St Joseph's Day), a very important date in the Catholic calendar. It is also my name day. Not many people realise that, because I am known to almost everybody as Pino, which is short for Giuseppe. San Giuseppe was a well respected and much admired saint and San Giuseppe Day used to be a Bank Holiday in Italy, when everything would be closed. It remains on the calendar but the Catholic Church has now abolished the Bank Holiday.

The day before San Giuseppe Day, my mother would go to our village shop to buy the ingredients she needed to make a traditional cake called Tarallo. This would be made only for special occasions like birthdays and name days. I remember arriving back home from school, walking into the kitchen and feeling the warmth coming from the oven. I would join my brothers and sisters around the kitchen table, eager to watch and help as my mother and my grandmother started making the cake.

First, a ring mould would be well greased and floured, then my grandmother would beat the eggs and the sugar in a large mixing bowl. My sister, Savina, would be allowed to add the fresh lemon rind and vanilla sugar and then all the other ingredients would be mixed together and baked in the ring mould, a wonderful aroma filling the kitchen when it was taken out and left to cool.

On the morning of San Giuseppe Day itself I would go to church with all the other children to attend Mass. The church would be packed to capacity on this particular day because the service was a special one. As it happened, our priest, Don Peppe, shared the same name as me, Peppe being another shortened version of Giuseppe. Towards the end of the service he would reach out his hand towards one side of the altar and produce a big, brown paper bag full of hard-boiled sweets. The sight of the bag excited us children among the congregation and Don Peppe would hand out two sweets to each of us as a little treat.

In Naples, they celebrate this day in a really big way. it is like an obsession with them - and an excuse for gluttony! They have even created a special sweet in honour of the saint - *Le Zeppole di San Giuseppe.* These small pastries are basically profiteroles. They are made out of choux pastry, which is piped onto a baking tray and then part-baked. As soon as the pastry rises, they are taken out of the oven and deep-fried in hot oil. At this stage the choux will puff out and double in size. They are then removed from the oil, drained over a piece of paper kitchen towel, hollowed out with a sharp knife and left to cool. Finally, they are filled with sweetened cream, flavoured with vanilla then dusted with icing sugar. Delicious! At home, my mother would make fresh tagliatelle to eat at lunchtime. She would also prepare the ingredients

MARCH

for her own, special, Bolognese sauce. The correct word in Italian for this sauce is *Ragù*. It is very rich when made properly but has to be cooked for a long time to give the perfect test. It is certainly worth waiting for. The union of the sauce and the tagliatelle is truly a marriage made in heaven!

To follow the pasta, there would be grilled chicken with rosemary (*pollo alla grilla con rosmarino*). I would go out into the piazza to look for my friends and invite them home. My mother, meanwhile, would have turned the Tarallo out onto a dish, dusting it with icing sugar. She would always wait for all my friends to arrive before slicing the cake. Glasses of orange and lemonade would then be filled to the top to wish me a happy name day.

Another great treat that my grandmother used to make for us children was a special yeast-baked cake. This would be baked in the shape of a doll (*la pupa*) for my sisters, Savina and Giovanna, and in the shape of a horse (*il cavalloo*) for me and my brothers, Lucio and Mario. I can still clearly remember the look of excitement on my sisters' faces when they saw my grandmother getting ready to mix the dough.

Concettina didn't have any proper moulds or pastry cuttters but simply modelled the dough into shape by hand. She was very artistic. The dolls had long bodies and round faces, the hands resting on the hips and the legs close together. The horses were also very cleverly done with long necks, ears and tails. While the dough was proving, Concettina would go to the fireplace and flick through the smouldering charcoal to find some tiny pieces of coal to place on the faces for eyes.

The cakes would then be taken to the village's public oven, where Inessa would bake them for us. "Hello, Concettina," she would say as we all came trooping in through the door. "You are just in time - the oven is ready!" Having popped the dolls and horses into the oven, Inessa, covered in flour, would flop down onto a small hand-finished rush chair to catch her breath, gazing up at the ceiling, scorched brown by the heat. Next to her, on the floor, there would be a basket full of dried twigs that she would throw onto the oven fire by the handful to keep it at the right temperature. She used to say that she could tell when the oven had reached the right heat for baking when

47

FLAVOURS OF ROSELLO

the bricks inside turned a precise shade of white.

Concettina, meanwhile, would stand beside her, using a wooden spoon to mix egg whites and caster sugar in a ceramic bowl with a wooden spoon until the mixture - which I only found out many years later was called meringue - turned white as snow (*il naspro*). When the baking was nearly done, the dolls and horses were taken out of the oven and the icing quickly poured over them. Tiny silver dragees were then sprinkled on them like little pearls before they were returned to the oven for a short time until the icing became crisp and hard. Of course, this sugar coating was the bit we liked most. Sweet and crunchy, the little silver balls glittered like tiny lights. Eaten on their own or dunked in milk, these cakes didn't last very long. We even had them for breakfast.

Another well-known, traditional speciality that we loved as children was *biscotti al ferro* (waffles). These have quite a rustic appearance, as they are never uniform in size and thickness. They used to be cooked on the embers of the open fire in heavy, rectangular, cast iron waffle moulds with long double handles, like old-fashioned fire irons. The design and pattern of the moulds were often a source of great family pride, featuring engraved names and coats of arms. These might vary from simple rows of lozenges and dots to the most complex geometric fantasies, the origins of which are said to go right back as far as the Arab mathematicians of old medieval Spain.

One of the finest sets of irons I have ever seen belonged to an uncle of mine, Ernesto. They included his grandfather's engraved initials and the family motto - '*omnis flamma at vitae*' (every flame is life). My sisters, Savina and Giovanna still make these biscuits, but instead of a log fire and some fine old waffle moulds they use modern electric waffle irons, which, I have to say, do the job just as well.

Savina and Giovanna make *biscotti al ferro* not just for themselves and their families, but also as presents to be given to friends and relations. It is such a lovely thing to do, I always think, to give a little present that one has gone to the trouble of making with one's own hands, rather than simply going into a shop to buy something that a machine has thrown together.

MARCH

Some years ago, I went to Belgium with my wife Caroline and our son Edilio, to stay with a dear French friend of ours, Catherine, who was working at the French Embassy as secretary to the ambassador in Brussels. I had been looking forward very much to visiting this great city and, in particular, to seeing the Grande Place, with its beautifully ornate, gilded buildings.

As well as admiring the many extraordinary examples of Gothic and Baroque architecture in the square, we also enjoyed doing a bit of window shopping. Brussels is, of course, famous for its chocolates and patisserie and some of the displays were mouth-watering. Edilio and I stopped for a drink at a coffee bar famed for its waffle biscuits. As soon as we walked in we were hit by the wonderful aroma of fresh roasting coffee while a large selection of gateaux and pastries were irresistibly displayed behind the thick, glass counter. The whole place was very cosy, with a lovely warm, friendly atmosphere. I sat down and ordered a coffee and waffle with vanilla ice cream while Edilio chose hot chocolate and a slice of lemon flan. The waffle was served warm, freshly cooked, and went perfectly with the ice cream.

Looking around, I was amazed to see that right opposite me, carefully arranged on the wall above an old mantlepiece, was a superb collection of fine old waffle irons. In a range of different sizes, large and small, they were decorated with some amazing patterns and I couldn't take my eyes off them as the childhood memories came flooding back.

FLAVOURS OF ROSELLO

TARALLO

This cake only used to be made by my mother on special occasions, such as on our birthdays and our name days. My sister Savina, who still makes it, gave this recipe to me.

4 eggs, size 4 lightly beaten
300g / 10 oz caster sugar
350g / 12 oz strong plain flour
200ml / 6 fl oz milk
200ml / 6 fl oz of oil ($1/2$ olive oil and $1/2$ cooking oil)
2 tsp baking powder
Rind of a lemon
A little vanilla essence

1 ring mould $1^{1}/4$ litre /2 $^{1}/4$pint or two small ones buttered and floured.

Beat the eggs and sugar with a whisk until the mixture has doubled in volume. In a fairly large bowl put the flour, the baking powder, milk, oil, lemon and vanilla. Whisk together. The mixture will become like a mass and fairly hard. Add the beaten eggs and mix the two together very well until they become a smooth liquid. Pour the mixture into the ring mould and bake on the middle shelf of the oven.

Leave to cool before unmoulding, and dust with icing sugar before serving.

Serves: 12
Preparation:: 20 minutes
Cooking: 45 minutes
Oven: 180°C/350°F/Gas 4

MARCH

SALSA BOLOGNESE or Ragù

The union of any kind of pasta and ragù is a marriage made in heaven! It is indispensable in lasagne dishes, and it is excellent with tagliatelle, spaghetti, penne, rigatoni and many others. When a menu lists alla Bolognese that means it is served with ragù.

1 small chopped onion
2 clove of garlic crushed
4 tbsp olive oil
2 tbsp finely chopped or grated celery
2 tbsp chopped or grated carrot
750g / 1 lb 8 oz minced beef (not too lean)
Salt. Freshly ground black pepper
250ml / $^1/_2$ pint dry red wine
2 whole cloves
1 bayleaf
1 tbsp tomato purée
800g / 1lb 12 oz tinned Italian tomatoes, chopped, with their juice
1 tbsp cornflour mixed with 2-3 tbsp of water.

In a heavy bottomed saucepan put the chopped onion, garlic and the oil and sauté briefly over a medium heat until transparent. Add the celery and carrot and cook for a further 2 minutes.

Add the minced beef, and stir to separate the meat. Add salt and pepper and cook until the mince has lost its raw, red colour. Pour in the wine, turn the heat up and cook, stirring until all the wine has evaporated.

Add the cloves, the bay leaf, tomato purée and the tomatoes with their juice, and stir thoroughly.

When the mixture has started to bubble, turn the heat down and cook the sauce by gently simmering. Cook uncovered, making sure to stir every now and then as the sauce could stick and burn easily. Thicken the sauce lightly with the cornflour to concentrate the taste. Taste and adjust seasoning.

Makes: 1 kg 400 / 3lb.1 oz
Serves: 6
Preparation: 20 minutes
Cooking 1 ½ hours

Chef's note: Ragù can be kept in the fridge for up to a week, or frozen. Reheat and simmer for about 15 minutes before using.

PEZZELLE AL FERRO
TRADITIONAL EASTER WAFFLES

Our mother used this recipe, which was kindly given to me by my sister Savina. It was a childhood treat, given to spoil us. The adults enjoyed it too.

For good waffle biscuits, I recommend an iron of a good make with grooves and pattern that are not too deep.

400g / 14 oz good plain flour
5 tbsp caster sugar
5 tbsp vegetable oil
4 eggs, size 4 lightly beaten
Juice of half lemon
2-3 pinches star anise powder

Put the flour on a working top. Make a well in the centre and then add the sugar, oil, lemon juice, anise powder and the eggs. Mix the ingredients with your fingers by drawing the flour into the centre to form a dough which must not be too soft, but malleable so as not to stick to your hands.

Cut the dough in half and roll to a sausage shape, then cut into pieces the

MARCH

size of small egg.

Heat the waffle iron and grease the grid with a kitchen towel dipped into a little oil.

Flatten the dough lightly with your fingers. Place the dough in between the hot plates and cook on both sides until lightly browned.

To serve: Sprinkle a little icing sugar over the waffles and eat them straight away or with a dollop of lightly whipped cream. They are much nicer when they are fresh, but they can be stored in an airtight tin box.

Makes: 16
Preparation: 15 minutes
Cooking: 30 minutes

FLAVOURS OF ROSELLO

AUNTY ANGIOLINA AND LE TAGLIATELLE

I remember this elderly lady very well. Short and a little plump, she talked through her nose and always dressed in black with a handkerchief over her head and tied under her chin.

The determination of this dear friend and elderly neighbour of ours went beyond every obstacle to please her daughter and her son-in-law. Aunty Angiolina used to visit her daughter in Switzerland and was very disappointed by the Swiss produce when she made her favourite home-made tagliatelle to please her family. On her return to the village she came around to see my mother. "Lina, when I was in Switzerland I made some tagliatelle which was a complete disaster. It was heavy, gluey and horrible, nothing like the ones we make here." But Aunty Angiolina would not give up. The next year she took one dozen fresh free-range eggs. Again another attempt failed! The year after that the dear lady took with her two kilos of our strong plain flour. But again it was not quite right.

The following year she filled up a large bottle of our fresh village water and took it all the way to Switzerland. It was a miracle. A success for our traditional dish and for Aunty Angiolina a big triumph - Viva Le Tagliatelle!

600g / 1lb 5 oz tagliatelle (dried will be fine unless you have the time and patience to follow Aunty Angiolina's example, and make it yourself!)
Tomato sauce (see recipe on page 42)
Parmesan cheese.

Fill a large saucepan with plenty of water, adding a little salt and a few drops of olive oil. Bring to the boil and cook the tagliatelle according to instructions. Simmer until almost tender and drain. Put the tagliatelle back into the saucepan, add a swirl of olive oil, some sauce and stir. Divide into portions. Add more tomato sauce and sprinkle with fresh Parmesan .
Serves: 6 - 8
Cooking time 20 minutes

APRIL

April dolce e dormire
April, how sweet to dream

In April, you always felt that spring was well and truly on its way. The warm sunshine would be accompanied by a festive mood as Easter approached. Palm Sunday (*La Domenica delle Palme*) is a very important religious date in our Calendar, the day when the olive branch is exchanged as a symbol of peace.

The village would turn out in force to attend Mass on a day that is regarded as being as special as Easter Sunday itself. My mother would send me to church with my brothers and my sisters, all dressed up in our best clothes, to collect the palm. The church pews would be filled to capacity and the service itself was a very solemn occasion, with flickering candles on the altar, the smell of incense, prayers for good health and the blessing of the olive branches that the Church Warden (*Sacrestano*) would hand out to each member of the congregation as they left afterwards. It was a moving occasion.

As well as peace, the exchange of palms was also meant to signify an end to minor grudges and there was one particular year when this was the cause of great merriment in our family. Despite living in the same neighbourhood, my aunts Gemma and Filomena had not been on speaking terms for many years. Returning from the church with her palm, Gemma went straight to Filomena's door and handed it to her, saying: "We are cousins and I have come to make peace with you. I think it is terrible that we don't even speak to each other. It is time to forget the past. Here is my palm - are you not going to give me yours in return?"

"I'm sorry, Gemma, I have been so busy this morning that I have not been to church," replied Filomena.

"So you don't want to make peace with me?"

"I told you, Gemma, I have no palm."

Gemma then snatched back her palm and stalked off, with a terse: "See you next year."

Easter week (*La Settimana Santa*) was our next school holiday after the Epiphany and, at last, we could have a week off to enjoy ourselves in the piazza and around the streets of the village. One of our favourite pastimes was to go round to Carluccio's Bar, where we would buy small chocolate Easter eggs and sweets and play pool. We would spend hours here, spending the pocket money our parents had given us.

The piazza was always busy, with people going to and fro or sitting on benches near the fountain. Around the piazza were two local food stores, two butcher's shops and a greengrocer, all doing good business as people stocked up with food for Easter. I remember going shopping with my grandmother, Concettina. Flavio Sammarone's general store would be full of Easter eggs of every imaginable size, wrapped up in the most beautifully coloured silver paper, some of them hanging from the ceiling on strings that stretched from one wall to another. Before deciding which one to buy, Concettina would ask Flavio to shake them hard, in turn, so that she could hear the sound of the surprise inside and try to work out which would be the most interesting.

The greengrocer was Saturno Monaco. His shop was always well stocked with every kind of fruit and vegetable, all of it beautifully and colourfully displayed. Angiolina, Saturno's wife, would serve us, gossiping all the while

APRIL

to Concettina.

On the way home, the most important stop would be at the butcher's shop of Vittorio D'Amico. A carcass hanging outside the door would signify that the new season lamb was in stock. Vittorio was a master butcher, affable and well liked by everyone. His shop was always spotlessly clean, cool and bright, with white tiles all around, and he himself was very helpful, suggesting what cut of meat to use for a particular dish.

Vittorio was born not in Rosello but in a village a few miles away called Quadri. His father and his two brothers were also butchers, each with a shop in a different village. It is a well-known fact that a good butcher father produces good butcher sons and Vittorio was no exception to this rule. At Easter we would invariably order two kilograms of leg of new season lamb as well as some cutlets, to be grilled on the hot charcoals from the fire.

During Holy Week Don Peppe would invite a monk from the nearby monastery to come and assist him in his duties. We children were very curious about the monk, with his long black beard hanging down almost to his chest, the brown frock down to his feet, the pure white cordons around his waist and his open sandals. He was very friendly and quite happy to chat with us and answer all our questions.

The highlight of the week's religious observances was the long procession of the Via Crucis, which would take place through the village streets on Good Friday, the men carrying the statue of Christ while the women prayed and carried a statue of the Madonna. The procession would stop twelve times, each time in a different street, when a passage from the bible would be read, signifying the twelve stations of the cross on Christ's journey to Calvary.

It was at this time of year that the men of the village, encouraged by their wives, their minds perhaps concentrated by the presence in our midst of the monk, would be moved to confess. It was as if this were a duty that had to be fulfilled at least once a year and so, rather reluctantly, they would drag themselves from the cantina on Easter Eve to unburden themselves. They actually found it a lot easier to make their confession to the monk, a relative stranger, than to old Don Peppe. An uncle of mine, Pasquale, went to confess

FLAVOURS OF ROSELLO

and the monk asked him: "Do you tell lies?" to which he replied: 'Father, we only survive by telling lies!"

Meanwhile, every effort was made to keep body, as well as soul, together. On Good Friday (*Venerdi santo*) we would usually have a traditional fish dish consisting of dried codfish, called *baccala*, which would be soaked in water overnight and then placed in a well-oiled oven dish and cooked in tomato sauce with sliced onions, chopped garlic and oregano.

A big treat at this time of year is our traditional Easter cake, the *Columba Pasquale*. This is a yeast cake, very light and with just enough mixed peel to give it a nice fruity taste. A few flaked almonds and sugar crystals are sprinkled over it before it is baked to give a lovely crusty topping. The cake is shaped like a dove, representing peace and the Holy Spirit, and no Easter meal is complete without it.

On Easter Sunday there would be a special festive meal. To start with, there would be a dish of home-made pasta with pesto sauce (*papardelle al pesto*) and, to follow, the leg of new season lamb would be roasted in the oven. In the afternoon we children would excitedly crack open our Easter eggs to reveal the surprise inside. Then my mother would bring in the *Columba Pasquale*.

Easter Monday (*Pasquetta*) was another festive day. It would usually be spent outdoors, weather permitting. People living in towns or cities would celebrate the day with another good meal before then going out for long walks (*passeggiata*) with family and friends. Folk like us, living in the country, would look forward to a picnic in the woods with an Easter pie (*torta pasqualina*) or maybe cold roast chicken and a chocolate and walnut cake (*torta di cioccolate e noci*).

My father, when he was home for Easter, liked to be a bit different from all the others so he would drag us all along to our orchard, which he had planted himself with the help of his cousin, Gesidio. He was very proud of his orchard. He had dug a well in one corner and had fitted it with a water pump that he bought in Rome. He had a little shed where he kept his tools and where he also had an old gas hob, with a gas cylinder, just in case he got

APRIL

peckish while he was working and wanted to heat up a snack. My mother didn't like to go to the orchard for a picnic because there would be nobody there except us - and she preferred to be with family or friends.

On the first Sunday after Easter Don Peppe would perform the ritual of blessing the houses. Dressed in his long black tunic, a white embroidered surplice and a velvety black hat with four rounded corners and a pompom in the middle, he would also be carrying his well-worn black leather Mass book. He would be followed by two young altar boys in red tunics and white surplices, one holding a silver filigree bucket with a shaker for the holy water and the other holding a leather pouch, with a brass slit in the top to put money in.

The blessing ceremonies would begin soon after lunch and each householder knew more or less what time Don Peppe would arrive. The ritual didn't take long. As soon as he walked through the door everyone would stand up and Don Peppe would open the mass book straight away and start reading the blessing in Latin, while the altar boy handed him the holy water to be splashed in the sign of the cross around the rooms. After the ceremony, a glass of red wine or Vermouth was offered to the priest and rarely refused, with biscuits for the altar boys, while money was put into the pouch. By the end of the day, Don Peppe had a soiled surplice and would be suffering from an overdose of hospitality. He was always quite shaky the following day.

Many years later, when I took Caroline home for the first time to meet my parents, we happened to be there on the day that this procedure took place. Ours was the first house visited and Caroline was touched and quite impressed by it all. Later in the afternoon we moved on to my grandmother's house to make our farewells, and our arrival co-incided with that of Don Peppe who was nearing the end of his long round of calls. By this time he almost had to be carried in, and his hastily spoken words were very slurred. Needless to say Caroline was very much amused.

April is also the month of wind and showers, and the time when the first wild snails are gathered. Together with neighbours and friends, we would go out in groups, buckets in hand, searching under stones and green foliage for

FLAVOURS OF ROSELLO

the small grey snails (*Halix Aspersa*) that are particularly good and succulent to eat. Sudden showers would send us all rushing for cover until it passed and the sunshine returned, often followed by a bright and colourful rainbow that would stretch from behind the mountain to a point deep down in the valley. As children, we would look up with great excitement, trying to count the seven beautiful soft colours on the clear background of blue sky.

We would take the snails back home where they would be left to starve for two to three days to purge them of any toxins. Concettina knew how to treat the snails to make them safe to eat, so they didn't make someone seriously ill. The purged snails first have to be washed five or six times in a mixture of salt, vinegar and water, after which they are blanched in boiling water for 10 minutes, cooled under running water and removed from their shells. The black fibres at the end of the snails are then removed and discarded, and the snails themselves cooked in a special stock. This is made by filling a stockpot with five litres of cold water, one carrot cut into thick slices, one onion cut in half, a few sprigs of thyme, two bayleaves, a good handful of fresh parsley and 60gm of salt. The shells must be washed, drained and left to dry in a warm oven or outside in the sun. Then they are ready for filling.

I remember how my mother, my grandmother and my neighbours would place a big cooper pot in the middle of the kitchen over a rolled up tea towel before sitting around to eat the great delicacy of snails in tomato and mint sauce (*lumache al pomodoro e menta*), which they would mop up with a lot of fresh bread.

The sauce would be made by frying some crushed garlic in olive oil, then added chopped tomatoes and their juice, then seasoning with salt and pepper. After simmering on a medium heat for about 20 minutes, they would then add the mint leaves and cook for a further five minutes.

If making this at home (and if you didn't want to find wild snails, then snails from a delicatessen would be fine), you would then place the snails inside the shells and arrange closely in an ovenproof dish. Pour the sauce over the snails, sprinkle over the chilli powder and bake in the oven for 10 minutes.

APRIL

TORTA PASCQUALINA
EASTER PIE

Frozen chopped spinach will do perfectly well for this recipe. Leave to defrost on a tea towel and squeeze out all the excess water.

500g / 1lb 2 oz chopped spinach leaves
60g / 2 oz fresh breadcrumbs
100ml / 3 fl oz milk
7 eggs, size 4
125g / 4 oz grated Parmesan cheese
250g / 8 oz fresh Ricotta or Mascarpone cheese
125g / 4 oz butter
250g / 8 oz packet large filo pastry sheets
3/4 tsp salt
15 grinds of freshly ground black pepper

Blanche the spinach leaves, drain well and cool under running water. Squeeze out the excess water and chop finely. In a bowl mix together the spinach, breadcrumbs and milk, and then stir in 2 of the eggs, Parmesan cheese and ricotta. Add the seasoning. Set aside.

Melt the butter and grease a 25 1/2 cm/10 inch loose-bottomed flan tin. Line with 2 sheets of filo pastry and brush with melted butter. Lay 2 further sheets of filo pastry over this, brushing each layer with melted butter taking care that the filo pastry overlaps the sides of the flan tin. Fill the flan tin with the spinach mixture and smooth the top.

Dip a tablespoon into melted butter and make five pockets in the mixture with the back of the spoon. Break an egg into each of the pockets and cover with the overlapping pastry. Brush again with more butter. Cut the remaining sheets of filo pastry in half and arrange them over the pie in an artistic way, again brushing with more melted butter, but taking care not to damage it.

Bake until the top is golden brown. Leave to stand for a little while before unmoulding it. Serve hot or bake it in advance and warm it up in the oven.

Serves: 8 or more
Preparation: 30 minutes
Cooking: 30-35 minutes
Oven: 180° C/350° F/Gas 4

PAPPARDELLE AL PESTO
PAPARDELLE WITH PESTO SAUCE

This classic and much-loved pasta dish is a gastronomic treat!

700g / 1 1/2 lb pappardelle pasta
60g / 2 oz of butter
Freshly grated Parmesan cheese
Freshly ground black pepper

Before beginning the pasta, prepare the pesto sauce using the recipe on the following page, it is worth the effort.

Take a large saucepan, fill it with plenty of hot water and bring it to the boil. Add a little salt and a few drops of olive oil. Cook the papardelle according to the instructions on the pack. When cooked, add 1 glass of cold water to prevent further cooking. Stir and strain. Return to the pan, add a knob of butter first, and then add the sauce. Mix well.

To serve: Dish the papardelle into individual plates and sprinkle with Parmesan cheese and a few rounds of black pepper.

Serves: 6
Cooking time: 12-15 minutes

APRIL

SALSA AL PESTO
PESTO SAUCE

60g / 2 oz fresh young basil leaves (no stems)
2 cloves of garlic
30g / 1oz pinenuts
10 tbsp olive oil
60g / 2 oz freshly grated Parmesan or a mixture of
Parmesan and Pecorino cheese

Shred the basil with your fingers. Put the nuts and garlic on a chopping board and cut into small pieces. For this a mezzaluna knife and a curved bowl are best or alternatively you can chop all three ingredients with a heavy knife and then tip them into a mortar to be crushed with a pestle. In this case add a few grains of sea salt to extract more flavour from the leaves, and reduce to a smooth green paste. Blend in half the oil, a spoonful at a time. Beat in the cheese; add the rest of the oil in a slow drizzle and season with more salt if necessary. Cover and leave for several hours before using to allow the flavours to blend and mature.

Serves: 6 or more
Preparation: 30 minutes

Chef's note:
To make one of my favourite pasta dishes, simply add to a little pesto one or two tablespoons of double cream (to make it smoother) before adding it to the pasta. On pizza before baking, pour a little pesto on to the base and spread it with the back of a spoon. The result is delicious. A chef colleague of mine, Giovanni, told me that in the Liguria di Levante a Rapallo, they add some Ricotta cheese to the pesto to make it more delicate, but they reduced the amount of Parmesan cheese.

FLAVOURS OF ROSELLO

ARROSTO DI AGNELLO PASQUALE CON VINO ROSSO
NEW SEASON'S ROAST LEG OF LAMB WITH RED WINE

It seems to be a tradition to serve lamb for the Easter Sunday lunch, here in England as well as in Italy. We always try to get the new season leg of lamb.

New leg of lamb weighing about 2.5kg / 5lbs
4 cloves of garlic
6 sprigs of rosemary
4 tbsp cooking oil
1 medium onion chopped
1 carrot peeled sliced
1 celery stalk chopped
Salt and freshly ground black pepper
200ml / 6 fl oz dry red wine
1.1 litres / 2 pint vegetable (carrot, leek) water

Score the fat on the leg of lamb. Slice 2 cloves of garlic and insert into the lamb with sprigs of rosemary. Crush the remaining garlic and place in the bottom of the roasting tin with the onion, carrot, and celery all mixed together.

Place the lamb on top, pour on the oil to coat all the sides and season well with salt and pepper. Roast the lamb for 30 minutes to give a good start and to brown the meat. Stir the vegetables so they do not burn. Lower the oven and add a little water if necessary to keep the vegetables moist and then continue cooking for a further hour.

Remove the roasting tin from the oven, place it directly over the heat, add the red wine and baste thoroughly. Lift the leg of lamb out, place on dish to keep warm.

Skim off as much fat as you can from the liquid. Remove the vegetables from the roasting tin. Add 5-6 level tablespoons of flour stir to make a roux.

APRIL

Add the warm vegetables stock, stir and bring to boil to thicken the gravy. Return the vegetables to infuse the flavours for a few moments. Serve with new minted potatoes.

Serves: 8-10
Cooking 1 hr 30 minutes
Oven: 200°C/400 °F/Gas 6   Then lower to: 170°C/325°F/Gas 3

TORTA DI CIOCCOLATA E NOCI
CHOCOLATE AND WALNUT CAKE

Let me to recount you a little story. I was working as a senior sous-chef at the Royal Trafalgar Thistle Hotel in Piccadilly. I was not only in charge of making the main courses but also on making desserts for the dining room. I had carte blanche, and could make whatever pudding I fancied and now and again I would produce this chocolate cake. One day the kitchen door sprang open and Sharon, the waitress, came in rather annoyed.

" Giuseppe come in the restaurant, a woman is having an orgasm after eating your chocolate cake and she wants your recipe." I went into the dining room to see the customer and she was raving about this chocolate cake. From then on it became known as the orgasm cake amongst the staff.

This extremely light Italian dessert has an unusual flavour and has been judged by my friends as exquisite.

150g / 5 oz walnuts
150g / 5 oz caster sugar
150g / 5 oz good quality chocolate melted
4 eggs, size 4 separated
A few drops of vanilla essence
Icing sugar to dust
A handful of breadcrumbs

With a pastry brush, thoroughly grease the inside of a 23cm / 9 in loose-bottomed cake tin. Sprinkle with plenty of breadcrumbs and icing sugar. Grind the walnuts, set aside, and then add the sugar, vanilla and melted chocolate. Mix well. Add the egg yolks and stir well. Beat the egg whites with a pinch of salt, but not too stiffly, so that they just form peaks. Add one third of the egg whites to the mixture and mix well.

Then fold the remainder of the egg whites into the ingredients very gently and pour into the cake tin. Bake in the oven and check with a skewer to see if it is cooked. The skewer must come out a little damp so that the cake is not too dry. When cold, tip out and dust with icing sugar.

Serves: 6 or more
Preparation: 20 minutes
Cooking: 30-35 minutes
Oven: 170°C/325°F/Gas 3

MAY

Una brava cuoca dispensa sapori e felicita
A good cook dispenses good meals and happiness

In the month of May, the countryside would be at its best, looking more beautiful than ever. The trees and hedges would be bursting with young foliage after the winter, and turning every shade of green; everything was growing and coming back to life, standing out against the still stark outline of the hills and surrounding landscape. I remember listening out for the muffled call of the first cuckoo, far away in the woods. The fields, meadows and banks would be thickly carpeted with golden yellow buttercups, dandelions and cowslips. Crab apple trees (*Malus sylvestris*) would be smothered in heavy pink blossoms. At home there were seeds waiting to be planted. May is truly a joyous month, the welcome prelude to the long, hot summer months to come.

As a very young boy I liked nothing better than to visit my aunt Concettina, my grandmother Felicetta and my cousin Lucia in their home at the other end of the village. I would make my way there along a narrow little pebbled

FLAVOURS OF ROSELLO

lane. On both sides of the lane there were shrubs and trees, thick, thorny brambles and small orchards belonging to the villagers. These orchards were no bigger than a couple of hectares of land but were tended with such loving care that it touched your soul.

They would be surrounded by makeshift fences, made from odds and ends of wood and barbed wire. At the entrance there would always be a little home-made gate, usually constructed from a few planks of wood roughly nailed together, with a piece of wire as a lock to stop anyone entering. Of course, anybody could still have walked in and taken whatever they wanted, but nobody ever did. Everybody knew and trusted each other.

My aunt's home was quite spacious, comfortable and cosy. You reached it through a little iron garden gate, walking along a path of stone slabs before going up a few steps to the front door. This led straight into the main living room, which was furnished with a wooden table and six hand-finished rush chairs, all neatly tucked under the table. There were no sofas or armchairs to sit down in, so whenever friends came to visit they would sit either around the table or on stools by the fire.

Felicetta kept the house beautifully tidy. The walls were whitewashed and there were old-fashioned floor tiles throughout the house. Two old pictures of hunting dogs, painted by an unknown Italian artist, hung on one wall alongside a glass mirror, with photographs tucked into the frame.

In the winter months, a lovely log fire was kept permanently burning in the white tiled fireplace at one end of the room. We would gather around it recounting events of the past, while the women were busy knitting socks or jumpers. Next to it they had a wooden stove to cook on, with a small water tank to one side. At the other end of the room stood a light wooden cabinet, with narrow shelves behind thick sliding glass, in which they kept the best china and glasses. A bottle of white vermouth and a packet of savoiardi biscuits were always ready to offer to visitors as a sign of good hospitality.

One autumn afternoon I went to visit them and found Felicetta and Concettina busy making marrow jam. There was great excitement and a bit of confusion because this was quite an unusual vegetable jam for them to be

MAY

making. Clean aprons were wrapped around their waists and large glass jars, ready sterilised, stood on the table, turned upside down.

On the stove, in a large, shining copper pot, the hot, bubbling jam was almost boiling over as the two women took turns to stir it continuously with a long-handled wooden spoon. Every now and again they would place a little of the hot liquid on a plate, to see if it was beginning to set. I was invited to have a taste, but quickly refused! I was too young then to be able to appreciate that what I thought of as a savoury vegetable could be turned into a delicious sweet jam with a wonderfully subtle taste. For my aunt and grandmother, who made it using marrows that they themselves had grown from seed, it was something special that they would be able to enjoy throughout the winter.

On summer afternoons from May onwards, they liked to sit in the garden in the shade of an umbrella tree that overhung the stepping stone path. Alongside this was a flowerbed that was a mass of colour throughout the summer, starting with bluebells, then tulips and pansies.

Although not very large, the kitchen garden was big enough to keep the household supplied with fresh vegetables throughout the summer. Square, with hedges all around, it was kept beautifully cultivated and not an inch of space was wasted. May was a busy month in the garden, with lots of potting, sowing and weeding to get on with.

Concettina and Felicetta always grew *zucchini* (courgettes) near the path, as they grow and spread very fast and cast shadows over the other plants with their giant umbrella leaves. Being near the path also made it easier to cut the fresh zuccini when they ripened. The colours of this lovely soft green vegetable with its orange flowers made it irresistible to eat. The flowers can be coated in batter and deep-friend (*fiori di zuccini fritti*) which is a great delicacy.

A strip of soil was reserved for beans, with a framework of tall wooden poles that they needed to climb up. The beans would be picked, shelled, freshly cooked and eaten with macaroni or in salads with tuna (*tonno e fagioli*). Some of the beans would left to dry out in the sun for use later in the year. Sweet corn was also grown in the garden, although sparingly. They would stand out from the other vegetables when fully-grown, reaching quite a height with their yellow cobs and long shining leaves. The corn was usually eaten boiled, cooked in a large copper pot over a log fire. It would take a few hours to cook, as everyone liked their corn tender, although personally, I always preferred my corn roasted over the embers, as it is tastier this way.

At the far end of the garden there was a small brick shed with a red terracotta tiled roof covered in sweet smelling roses that climbed and grew all over it in a wild rambling fashion. This shed had a green painted wooden door, which was always open in the summer days in order to keep the inside cool. Here was kept everything from firewood to garden tools, with dried bunches of oregano suspended from the ceiling, strings of garlic and onions hanging on the wall and green tomatoes ripening slowly. There were also all manner of other odds and ends that intrigued me so much that I would spend hours in that shed, looking around in the hope of discovering some hidden treasure inside an old box or a basket stuck in the corner.

MAY

INSALATA DI TONNO E FAGIOLI
TUNA AND BEAN SALAD

This is a delicious way to use fresh beans with tuna to make a tasty and delightful Italian salad.

200g / 7 oz cooked beans. Use red kidney beans, borlotti, cannellini or other similar tinned beans and always rinse thoroughly.
1 small onion finely chopped
200g / 7 oz tinned tuna in olive oil or brine, drained
5 tbsp olive oil
2-3 tbsp white wine vinegar
Salt and freshly ground black pepper
2 tbsp freshly chopped parsley

If using dried beans, soak overnight. Rinse and drain the beans, boil in fresh water for 10 minutes. Rinse and drain again then boil once more in plenty of cold water with half an onion, 1 small carrot, 1 celery stalk, crushed garlic, salt, a sprig of parsley and swirl of olive oil. Cook until tender. This could take as long as 4 hours depending on the beans.

Drain the beans and when cold put them in a salad bowl. Add the chopped onion and season with salt to taste. Add the tuna, breaking it into large flakes with a fork. Add the olive oil, vinegar and a few rounds of pepper. Toss thoroughly. Sprinkle with parsley and serve. If you don't like or want tuna, it can be omitted without ruining the salad in any way.

Serves: 6
Preparation: 25 minutes

Chef's note: You can serve this salad with grilled and barbecued meat.

FLAVOURS OF ROSELLO

POLLO ALLA DIAVOLA
DEVILLED CHICKEN

Do not hesitate on the mustard, or it will not be *alla diavola* 'hot as the devil' and never serve this dish if you invite a Catholic priest for a meal!

2 spring chickens, weighing 1kg / 2 lb 2 oz
2-3 tbsp English mustard, prepared or powder
4 slices fresh breadcrumbs coarsely ground (remove crusts)
90g / 3 oz melted butter
2 springs of fresh thyme
Salt and 1 bunch of watercress

Prepare the chickens and truss them by slipping the drumsticks into incisions made in the skin on either side. Cut the connective tissue at the leg joints to make it lie flat when the heat touches it. Split the chicken from neck to tail down the back, open it out and flatten lightly with a wooden mallet. Season with salt. Place in a roasting pan; baste with melted butter and sprigs of thyme and roast in the oven, skin side up and roast the skin has turned well brown and crisp. Half way through cooking remove the chickens from the oven. Brush or spread on both sides with mustard. Sprinkle the breadcrumbs on both sides and press down with a palette knife. Turn it over skin side up. Baste with the melted butter. Finish cooking in the oven to crisp the breadcrumbs, ensuring that it does not burn. Cut into portions and garnish with watercress.

Serves: 6 or more
Cooking: 30-35 minutes
Oven: 190°C/375°F/Gas 5
This chicken recipe comes from among my early recollections, going back to my years in the kitchen at the Belgian Embassy in Rome, when the Chef Eduardo Coletta used to prepare it for the Ambassador and his family.

MAY

FIORI DI ZUCCHINE FRITTI
FRIED COURGETTE FLOWERS

If you grow your own courgettes, cut off the blossoms from the plants. They make a delicious and delectable vegetable that is extremely simple to prepare.

3-4- courgette flowers per head or some very small baby courgettes
Cooking oil for frying
For the batter:
200g / 7 oz plain flour
2 tbsp olive oil
2 eggs, size 1, separated
Salt
200ml / 6 fl oz cold water

Put the flour in a bowl, and then add the olive oil, egg yolks and salt. Add the cold water, a little at the time, to make a smooth, but not too liquid batter. Stir well and leave to rest for half an hour. Beat the egg whites with a pinch of salt until they form soft peaks. Fold the egg whites into the mixture. It is now ready to use.

Put the deep fryer on the heat and leave it to get warm. You want a temperature of 190°C/375°F to seal the crust or to set the batter, and to prevent too much oil being soaked up. To check whether the oil is hot enough put a piece of bread in and it will show you how quickly it will brown. Wipe the courgette flowers with a kitchen cloth. Coat the flowers by dipping them a few at the time into the batter and then fry them in the hot oil. Turn them over with a slotted spoon, lift them out and drain on kitchen paper. Add a sprinkle of salt and serve with lemon quarters cut lengthways.

Preparation: 15-20 minutes
Chef's note: Serve the flowers as soon as they come from the fryer, or the batter will become soft and lose its crispness.

SPAGHETTI CON PISTACCHI E BASILICO
SPAGHETTI WITH PISTACHIOS AND SWEET BASIL

125g / 4 oz spaghetti
30g / 1 oz butter
60m / ¹/₂ fl oz double cream
15g / ¹/₂ oz pistachios, roughly chopped
2 large or 4 small fresh leaves of sweet basil, roughly chopped
Freshly ground black pepper
Freshly grated Parmesan cheese

Take a large saucepan, fill it with plenty of hot water and bring it to the boil. Add a little salt and a few drops of olive oil. Cook the spaghetti according to instructions.

While the spaghetti is cooking, prepare the sauce. Melt the butter in a frying pan, add the double cream and bring lightly to the boil. Add the pistachios and sweet basil, and gently cook for a few minutes until all the flavours infuse. Add a few rounds of black pepper to taste.

When the spaghetti is cooked, add 1 glass of cold water to prevent further cooking, stir and strain. Return to the pan and pour the sauce over the hot strained spaghetti. Mix and serve with Parmesan cheese.

Serves: 1
Preparation: 5 minutes
Cooking: 15 minutes

Chef's note: If you prefer the spaghetti runnier, add a little olive oil when returning the pasta into the saucepan, and then add the sauce.

MAY

SALMONE AFFUMICATO
SMOKED SALMON

This recipe was very kindly given to me by Mr John C Watkinson, Consultant Otolaryngologist /Head and Neck Surgeon.

2 large sides of fresh salmon (wild or farmed)
2-3 tablespoons of sea salt
A good handful of fresh dill or 1 tbsp dried
2-3 tablespoons of molasses
2-3 tablespoons of brown sugar
1 bottle of British cream sherry or Whisky (optional)

Wash the fish in cold water, then pat dry and cover the bottom of a large oval dish with sea salt. Lay the salmon skin down, and sprinkle with chopped dill and cover the top of the salmon with more salt, brown sugar and molasses. Repeat the same on the other side of salmon. Leave for six hours to form brine.

Transfer the fish into a prepared container filled with a bottle of British cream sherry or a bottle of Whiskey, if you prefer. Leave for 4-6 hours. Dry and leave overnight. Smoke for 4-6 hours using hard wood chippings.

Serves: One side of smoked salmon for 12 people
Preparation: 1 hour
Curing time: 4-6 hours
Smoking time: 4-6 hours

Mr John C Watkinson is a Consultant Surgeon with a busy practice and fishing is one his favourite ways of relaxing. He most enjoys catching a fresh salmon, smoking it himself and then eating it with home made bread.

FLAVOURS OF ROSELLO

SEMIFREDDO AL GRAND MARNIER
ICED GRAND MARNIER SOUFFLÉ

A cold, uncooked delicious soufflé that can be kept in the freezer.

10 egg yolks eggs size 4
200g / 7 oz sugar
2 tbsp water
1 vanilla pod
4 tbsp Grand Marnier
500ml / 16 fl oz double cream
5 egg whites, beaten
2 tbsp cocoa powder

Encase the soufflé dish in a double layer of greaseproof paper, about 5cm/2 inches higher than the edges of the dish and secure with string. Keep the dish in the fridge.

Put the egg yolks, vanilla pod and water in a large bowl over a pan of hot water or on top of a double boiler. Beat the mixture over the hot, but not boiling, water until the eggs have doubled and are a pale straw colour. Draw off the heat and stir, ensuring that the mixture becomes completely cold.

Add the Grand Marnier, the lightly whipped cream and the beaten egg whites (not too stiff). Fold all the ingredients very gently together, and pour into the soufflé dish. Place in the freezer and leave for several hours or overnight.

Before serving, dust with cocoa powder and remove the greaseproof paper.

This ice cream can be served with hot chocolate sauce, but in this case do not dust with the cocoa powder.

Serves: 6 or more
Preparation: 10 minutes
Beating and finishing: 45 minutes

JUNE

Il tempo e la memoria
The time and the memory

June was always my favourite month, with the school year drawing to a close and the summer holiday *(le grande vacanze)* approaching. Like schoolboys everywhere, I was always eager to see the school front door shut at the end of another year.

From the middle of June until the beginning of October we would have one long holiday and I would spend almost every day out in the open, dressed in shorts, t-shirts and sandals. One year I remember my mother bought me a pair of red sandals. She liked them because she thought they were pretty, but I was too shy to wear them because my friends would tease me and say that they were girl's sandals.

We knew the shoe-seller as *La Parigina*. The Parisienne. She was married to an Italian and they lived a few kilometres away in the town of Villa Santa Maria. How she came to live in that part of the world I don't know, but most probably her husband must have worked in France, swept her off her feet and

FLAVOURS OF ROSELLO

taken her away from that beautiful city to return back to his roots. Early in the morning they would set up their stall in the piazza, piling up box upon box of shoes, the left shoe placed on top of the last box, to show off the style and the latest fashion. There was a small rush chair beside the stall and here, amid a melée of the mothers and children, we would sit to try the new shoes on.

La Parigina was a very well-known lady with a great charm. She spoke Italian, but with a strong French accent. I don't remember my mother or any others ever calling her by her Christian name. She called my mother Lina, as she knew her well, but my mother always addressed her as signora. I don't think anyone bothered to find out her Christian name. She was La Parigina and she sold good strong shoes that lasted well and that was all that mattered.

We children whiled away the long hot days of summer with all sorts of games, including football, netball and something called mazza e pizzotte, which is a bit like cricket. We used to visit friends in surrounding villages on foot. Often it would be so hot that in the afternoons we would go and bathe in the nearby river, the Turcano. Deep in the valley, this river was surrounded on all sides by mountains whose slopes were thickly wooded with oak and elm trees. I wasn't happy in the water so I never learnt to swim, but just watched as my friends bathed in the pools that had formed on the riverbed.

On the way, we would stop to drink water from an old fountain (la fonte vecchia), whose crystal clear water was renowned for making you feel good due to its purity and lightness. Until the mains water pipes were installed in our village in the 1950's there were no street fountains and the women used to walk about one kilometre to la fonte vecchia to fetch water in copper pots, carrying it back home on their heads.

There were several special dates in the June calendar. On June 13th, for instance, my grandmother would always be invited to the nearby village of Borrello by our relations, Aunt Lucia and Uncle Guglielmo, to join in the saint's day celebrations for the village's patron saint, St. Antonio, and she used to take me with her for company. There was a bus that went to Borrello, but it would arrive very early, making the day too long and tiring, so we would

JUNE

walk there instead, setting off around mid-morning.

When we finally arrived, Uncle Guglielmo and his family would welcome us with a delicious slice of cherry flan (*crostato di ciliege*) served with a fresh cup of coffee. I would then sit quietly in one corner of the room, resting my legs from the journey, while my grandmother would catch up with all the current news and gossip.

Outside in the streets, the villagers would be in festive mood. In the centre of the piazza, chairs would be placed around the bandstand, ready for people to listen to the band playing later in the evening. There would be stalls selling souvenirs, toys, balloons, also games with water pistols and rifle shooting. A big carousel spun around with brightly painted chairs carrying children who held their breath as they flew through the air. Because this was a religious day, there would also be a Mass and a procession, with a large brass band wearing dark blue uniforms. An effigy of the saint would be carried on men's shoulders while all those watching sang and prayed.

What I was really looking forward to most was the chance to taste the first red cherries of the season. Those cherries were far more important to me than the saint! Reaching into my short trousers pocket, I would search for a few lire and, feeling a little shy, I would hand it over to the vendor who would place a handful of cherries on a square piece of paper and give it to me. Soon after that, men on donkeys would come to our village, too, with their wicker baskets filled up to the top with ripened red cherries. They would sit next to the little drinking fountain in the piazza, selling them by the kilo.

Haymaking was another important event in June. All the meadows that surrounded the village were kept purely for haymaking and, shortly before it was time to cut the hay, they would be covered in buttercups, looking as if they had been painted a vibrant yellow. The hay would be cut using a scythe, sharp as a razor. The man using it would move through the field at a steady pace, each stroke following the same direction as the last, leaving a series of neat semi-circles behind him. A lonely figure, lost in the midst of the waist-high grass, he was very much part of our early summer landscape. At that time of the year the air would be full of the characteristically pungent smell

FLAVOURS OF ROSELLO

of freshly cut hay. As a lad, I used to visit some farmer friends, the Caracino family, to help them rake in the hay for storage. It was a fun day, different to the others, and I loved to get together with the family and share in their enthusiasm.

The hay had to be raked and then lifted with a wooden fork onto a rope net that had two long poles at both ends. When the net was full, the ends would be tied into a huge roll, loaded onto a saddled mare, and transported back to the stable. It was hard, tiring work and the sweat would pour down your face in the intense heat. At midday, I felt a great relief when one of the families would bring food and wine for us and we would sit in the shade of a wild pear tree (*pyrus cordata*) to eat our lunch. I remember with great pleasure resting, chatting and admiring the yellow flowers of the Ginestas on the hillside in front of us.

In June of 1957, on Corpus Domini day, I received my first communion and confirmation (*La prima communione e crestima*), together with my sister, Savina, and my brother, Lucio. We had been putting this off, year after year, in the hope that there would be a time when my father could be there for this special occasion, but being on board the warships meant that it was difficult for him to get leave at the right moment in June. In the end, my mother made the big decision that we would have to go ahead without him. She went to see our priest, Don Peppe, to explain the decision she had taken, and he suggested that we joined the other children for the afternoon Catechism lessons at the church.

It was going to be hard work to learn about the spiritual and charitable works of the Catechism. We had to be able to recite them by heart and Don Peppe would put us to the test with constant interrogations. He was worried that, on the day of the confirmation, Il Vescovo the Bishop Monsignor Crivellari (strange that even after so many years, I still remember his name - it might be because in our dialect language his name means 'sieve'!) might ask us questions about the Catechism and that if we did not answer properly it would have been very embarrassing for Don Peppe in a church filled with his parishioners. A few years earlier, when the Bishop asked a question, a child had replied, "The priest has not taught it to me," and the entire congregation laughed.

I was equally embarrased about having to hold hands with my friend Antonio during the procession around the village. Antonio was the same age as me and in the same class at school. We are still friends today and he, too, is a chef. I often used to go to his house on my way home, where his parents

Orlando and Gilda, lived with Gilda's Aunt Lucia and Uncle Carmine. Aunt Lucia, always dressed in black, was old and frail and hard of hearing with poor eyesight as well and when I arrived in the house she would demand: "Who are you? Who are you?" And I would shout back" "I am the grandson of Concettina Della Storna."

La Storna was the nickname originally given to my great-grandmother - on my mother's side. This was because at an early age all her hair had turned white, and she used to wear a very long plait. She also owned a pure white mare, and at that time a poem had been written called La Cavallina Storna (a white young mare). My great-grandmother was nicknamed after this poem.

"You know we are related too, don't you?" Aunty Lucia would say with a chuckle.

FLAVOURS OF ROSELLO

"Yes, I know Aunty Lucia," I would say wearily, knowing what was coming next.

At this point, Antonio's mother would turn around with her hands on her hips and say to me: "Pino, did you know that when you were a little baby I used to breastfeed you? Your mother lost all her milk, and I fed for you for several months."

"I know, I know," I would reply, blushing.

Every time I went there with Antonio I was always kindly reminded of this story and Aunty Lucia would tell me how we were related. At the time my mind was too busy with other things and, anyway, I was too young even to understand all the connections. Perhaps I should have taken more notice then, but alas, it is too late now.

Antonio and I were good friends and we had to be even better friends if we were going to hold hands together at our first Communion! This was a very serious time in my life and I was never going to forget it. Ercolino, the tailor from the next village, Borrello, came to our house to take the measurements for our confirmation outfits. There were shiny, silvery suits for me and my brother and a white dress for my sister. On top of that there were white arm bands with gold engraved chalices, gold initials on the white ties and white pocket handkerchiefs for us boys. And for all of us there were white gloves, white prayer books, a white rosary, white socks and shoes.....it was almost as if we were going to get married!

At the last moment came a surprise. Don Peppe asked to see my mother and told her he was disappointed and not happy with Lucio's Catechism.

"I am not willing to confirm Lucio, he does not know enough!"

My mother implored Don Peppe. "I have already bought the suit," she said. "Maybe if you put him at the back behind the other children the Bishop will not see him and will not ask him any questions. Please, Don Peppe, I will bring you a special cake and a bottle of brandy so you can offer it to the Bishop after the ceremony." She knew the way to our old priest's heart!

The day before the ceremony, we all had to go to confess and repent of our sins. Each one of us in turn then had to say the Credo, a few Gloria Al Padres,

JUNE

and recite the Ave Maria. We had to be careful not to swear if we got it wrong, otherwise we had to go back to confess again, because the day after we were going to receive Jesus Christ.

As a Celebration day treat we would have sponge cakes filled with two pastry creams made of vanilla and chocolate. The sponge is cut horizontally into three slices, sprinkled with sugar syrup flavoured with liqueurs, garnished with the pastry creams and finished off with fresh whipped cream and candied fruit peel. A dear friend of my father, Pietro, had kindly made them for us. He also had made a big sponge cake especially for Don Peppe, the top decorated with the three crosses of Calvary to impress the Bishop.

On the morning of the big day the sun was shining and it looked as if it was going to be a beautiful day. The church bells rang out and everyone was very excited. All the boys were smartly dressed and the girls, looking angelic walked in front of us. The entire village was out there in the piazza, waiting to see the Bishop, and by the time he arrived we were already shaking with fear. What would he look like? What sort of questions was he going to ask? We were not praying to receive Jesus Christ, only that the Bishop would not ask any questions at the altar!

In his highly embroidered silk robes, the Bishop celebrated Mass and then the procession began around the village, with all of us in a crocodile, holding hands and singing religious songs. Just then dark clouds appeared above the mountains, the sky turned black and by the time we arrived back at the church it was raining so hard that everybody was rushing to get inside. Then the heavens opened even more violently, with thunder, lightening, hailstones and torrential rain. The village was nearly washed away! The Bishop had the fear of God on his face; he had never seen anything like it. He rushed to complete the service and could not get out of the church fast enough, so we got away without a single question being asked! This went down a treat for all of us, including Don Peppe. Not only had no awkward questions been asked but there was the delicious cake waiting to be eaten!

FLAVOURS OF ROSELLO

LINGUINI AI FRUTTI DI MARE
LINGUINI WITH SEA FOOD

The best-known and most popular dish on the southern coast of Italy is spaghetti with shellfish (it's usually *clams-vongole*) where some restaurants like to serve the pasta with mussels and clams in their shells. The freshness, the smell of the ingredients, and the presentation with fresh flat parsley is unique.

500g / 1 lb 2 oz linguini
500g / 1 lb 2 oz mussels
300g / 10 oz clams
100g / 4 oz prawns peeled
6 tbsp olive oil
2 cloves garlic, chopped
350g / 12 oz chopped peeled tomatoes
100ml / 3 fl oz dry white wine
2 tbsp fresh chopped parsley
Salt and freshly ground black pepper
Chopped parsley to garnish

Wash the clams and the mussels, remove beards and barnacles and scrub with a brush. Discard any broken shells and those that do not close when they are tapped. Put them in a covered large pan, with a glass of water, over a high heat until they open. Remove the mussels from their shells (throw away any that do not open). Strain their juices through a fine sieve and keep aside.

Fry the chopped grlic in oil, and when it begins to colour add the chopped tomatoes, the strained mussel juices and the wine. Boil vigorously to reduce the liquor, and then add the clams, the mussels and prawns. Sprinkle with salt and pepper and cook for a few minutes longer. The fish needs only to be heated through.

84

JUNE

Cook the linguini in plenty of boiling salted water (read instructions for cooking time). Drain the linguini quickly when it is only just tender (*al dente*), return to the pan, cover with the sauce and sprinkle with parsley. Do not serve with Parmesan cheese.

Chef's note: If you prefer, you can adapt this recipe with spaghetti or vermicelli, and other shells like sea dates, shrimps and calamari.

Serves: 6 or more
Preparation: 20 minutes
Cooking time: 20 minutes - plus time for the pasta

FLAVOURS OF ROSELLO

RISOTTO ALLA MILANESE CON ZAFFERANO
SAFFRON RISOTTO

100g / 4 oz butter
4 tbsp olive oil
1 medium onion, finely chopped
500g / lb 2 oz Italian rice
100ml / 3fl oz dry white wine
1½ litre / 3 pints hot chicken or vegetable stock
2g saffron, or a small bag
4 tbsp fresh grated Parmesan cheese
Salt and freshly ground black pepper

In a heavy-based saucepan heat half the butter and the oil. Add the finely chopped onion and fry until transparent but not brown. Add the rice, stir with a wooden spoon and fry for 2 minutes over a brisk heat. Add the wine and leave to infuse.

Add 1-2 ladles of the hot chicken stock. Simmer gently and stir with a wooden spoon to loosen the grains of rice. When the stock begins to absorb, add more but do not let it get dry. Continue simmering and add further hot stock every 5-6 minutes until it is cooked. The rice must remain soft and runny . Continue to stir occasionally. Towards the last five minutes add the saffron and adjust seasoning. The risotto is done when is tender but firm to the bite (*al dente*). Add the remaining butter and all the cheese and mix thoroughly. Spoon into a hot dish and serve with a bowl of freshly grated Parmesan cheese.

Serves: 6
Preparation: 10 minutes
Cooking: 20 minutes

JUNE

INSALATA D'ESTATE
SUMMER SALAD

This is a crisp and colourful salad with a refreshing taste.

2 large segmented oranges
1 medium radicchio lettuce, washed, separated and drained
2 chicory
1 good handful of small sorrel lettuce, washed and drained
4 tbsp walnut oil
A dash of balsamic vinegar
Salt and freshly ground black pepper.

Cut the chicory obliquely into half-inch slices. Remove the stalks from the sorrel. Cut the larger radicchio leaves in half.
In a bowl, combine the oil, balsamic vinegar, seasoning and orange segments. Add the washed lettuce leaves and toss them in the oil and orange dressing. Arrange the salad on individual plates or in a glass bowl.

Serves: 6
Preparation: 15 minutes

FLAVOURS OF ROSELLO

SCALOPPINE DI SALMONE CON RUCHETTA
SALMON ESCALOPES WITH ROCKET SAUCE

A rich and elegant main course that is light and tasty and ideal for a summer dinner party.

6 thinly sliced escalopes of fresh salmon, each weighing about 200g / 7 oz
2 tbsp olive oil
Salt and freshly ground black pepper
A little paprika

Use one fillet of salmon weighing about 1.3kg / 3 lb and cut horizontally (as for smoked salmon) into 6 equal slices of 200g / 7 oz. Alternatively, ask the fishmonger to fillet it for you. Place each slice between 2 sheets of cling-film and flatten them gently. Place a piece of foil on a baking tray that is large enough for all 6 escalopes. Brush the fish with olive oil, season with salt and pepper, dust with paprika and set aside.

Bake the salmon in the oven for about 2 minutes. Do not overcook it.

To serve: Pour a little sauce on each plate and arrange a salmon escalope on top. Serve the remaining sauce on the side.

Serves: 6
Preparation: 10 minutes
Oven: 200°C/400°F/Gas 6

Chef's note: The escalopes can also be cooked very fast - just a few seconds on each side - in a little hot oil in a frying pan. Take care not to let them become dry.

JUNE

SALSA DI RUCHETTA
ROCKET SAUCE

1 small onion finely chopped
l oz butter
100ml / 3 fl oz dry white wine
300ml / ¹/₂ pint fish stock
300ml / 9 fl oz double cream
1 handful rocket leaves
A little lemon squeeze
Salt
Freshly ground black pepper

Beurre manié

60g / 2 oz butter, softened and mixed with
60g / 2 oz plain flour

Remove the stalk from the rocket leaves with the scissors. In a small saucepan, gently sauté the onion in the butter for a few minutes or until soft. Add the wine, then, boil the liquid for 5 minutes to reduce it to thin syrup. Stir in the fish stock. Bring the liquid back to boil then continue to boil to reduce it a little further. Add the cream to the pan to boil and simmer the sauce for another 5 minutes. Mix the butter and flour to make the beurre manié and add to the sauce a little at the time to thicken slightly, whisking until the sauce is smooth. You may not need all the beurré manie. Add a few drops of lemon juice and adjust seasoning to taste. Sieve into a clean pan. Sweat the rocket leaves lightly in a saucepan with a knob of butter and little seasoning. Add the rocket leaves to the sauce.

89

FLAVOURS OF ROSELLO

CROSTATA DI CILIEGE
CHERRY TART

This is one of my favourite flans. The cherries remind me of the beginning of the summer and I enjoy eating it not only when the flan is cold, but also warm at room temperature dusted with icing sugar and a swirl of cream.

Sweet shortcrust pastry (for recipe see page 141)

For the filling:
1 kg / 2 lb 4 oz fresh cherries, stoned
125g / 4 oz unsalted melted butter
125g / 4 oz icing sugar
125g / 4oz ground almonds
2 eggs, size 4, lightly beaten
1 tbsp plain flour
1 tbsp Maraschino or kirsch (optional)
6 tbsp redcurrant jelly to glaze

With a pastry brush, grease the inside of a tart tin and dust with flour. Roll out the pastry to about 1/2 cm/ 1/4inch thick and line a loose-based flan tin of 23cm/9 inch diameter ensuring that the pastry is even. Trim off any surplus and press the edges of the flan dish with your fingers to raise the pastry a little higher than the edges. Prick with a fork and bake blind for 15 minutes. Stone the cherries, rinse under running cold water, pat dry and set aside. Melt the butter over a low heat and allow to cool. Mix the butter in a bowl with the icing sugar, ground almonds, eggs and flour. Spread the mixture in the flan case, arrange the stoned cherries over this and bake in the oven.

When cold, melt the redcurrant jelly with the liqueur and brush over the flan to give an even glaze.

Serves: 6 or more
Preparation: 30 minutes
Cooking: 25-30 minutes
Oven: 170°C/325°F/Gas 3 for pastry, then: 180°C/350°F/Gas 4 for filling.

JULY

Il fruttivendolo chiama la clientela di venire a comprare
The fruit vendor calling the customer to come and buy

In the month of July the red poppies could be seen everywhere, stretching out in never-ending lines. There were clumps of bright, dazzling colour by the side of our old stone church and on the corners of our village streets. Across the open green countryside they punctuated the wheat and barley with their bright yet soft, delicate petals.

The ripe wheat, now fully mature, would be turning golden brown in the hot July sun, ready for the harvest. This was all done by hand, often in the most difficult and sloping parts of the countryside. On every piece of land, as far as the eye could see, there would be a peasant farmer cutting the straw. It took a long time using just a sickle, a slow and backbreaking task. The men worked alongside each other, bent down towards the dry earth, occasionally exchanging a few words and stopping for a moment to rest their aching backs.

My most vivid memories are of the times when one of the harvesters would

FLAVOURS OF ROSELLO

suddenly start to sing a bar of one of our folk songs, in time to the rhythm of the sickles cutting the wheat. An instant choir would be formed, singing with such harmony and high spirits that the echo resounded and could be heard for miles, all around the neighbouring fields. I can hear it now in my head.

All the farmers would get themselves organised in plenty of time for the harvest, asking relations, friends and neighbours for help. They would then set out early in the morning, walking to the fields to start the long day. The harvest meant a great deal of hard work for everyone, as well as the reliance on friendship for a helping hand.

During July, I would regularly go to spend three weeks in Pescopennataro, another village just a few miles away. The village is built on a hilltop, with an incredible panoramic view that extends for miles, right across the surrounding valleys. At an altitude of 4,000 feet above sea level, there is always a cool breeze in the evening even during the hottest summer days.. The next village, Capracotta (the name means cooked goat!) was even higher at an altitude of 4,500 feet, and is the highest and coldest place in the Molise Region. During the winter months, the snow would be as high as the houses!

My father's relatives lived in Pescopennataro and, very kindly, used to invite me to spend a holiday with them. Uncle Gesidio was my father's cousin and he and his wife, Aunty Linda had a grown up family. When I was a young boy, my mother was concerned that I looked too pale, too thin and too skinny for my age, so she would send me to stay with them for three weeks in the hope of getting some colour back into my cheeks. She thought it would do me the world of good, especially with all that fresh air going through my lungs. And she was right. I always went back home revitalised.

I eventually got to know most of the people in Pescopennataro so well that I was almost one of them. I made many friends and I would go out and take part in the village sports events with children of my own age. In the afternoons I would play outside in the friendly neighbourhood, chatting with passers-by in the narrow cobbled street where my uncle lived.

Uncle Gesidio was the village municipal guard and gamekeeper. He held that job for years, as long as I can remember, and kept on doing it until his

JULY

retirement. Sometimes he would walk over to visit us at Rosello. He enjoyed walking through the countryside, with his double barrel gun over his shoulder, keeping an eye out for field mushrooms to bring to us as a gift.

Once, it must have been in the autumn, he came over on a day when there was the most miserable weather outside, cold, wet and windy. My mother's sister-in-law, Felice, who lived just down the road, had also popped in for a quick visit and a chat. Felice had the habit of sitting as close to the fire as she could get and after a while she said to my mother: "Lina, there is a funny smell in the house, as if something is burning, I think it could be the soot." She then knelt on one knee, and steadying herself with one hand on the fireplace, peered up the chimney. Sure enough, the soot was on fire.

The panic that followed was incredible and we were all frightened. Like any inquisitive child, I had to have a look myself to make sure Felice was right. I peered up and saw this red glow, as if there was a red moon sitting on top of the chimney. Meanwhile, my mother and grandmother were imploring the help of the Madonna della Libera (the Madonna of freedom) to save us from disaster. Gesidio then had the brilliant idea of blazing the soot with his double barrel gun! He must have thought that by shooting the soot he would be able to bring it down in one piece and that would be the end of it. He loaded the gun and my grandmother gave him a white towel to cover his head, so that he reminded me of a boxer, entering the ring for a fight.

More panic and more Madonnas! Gesidio positioned himself, with one knee bent on the floor, the gun pointing up the chimney. We all stepped back and covered our ears with our hands and then suddenly he pulled the trigger. An almighty bang shook the whole house and we all jumped in the air, but, unfortunately, his idea did not work. In fact it simply made things worse, igniting more of the soot.

The panic was even greater now and Felice ran out to ask our neighbours for help. I was desperate to go outside to see what was going on amid all the commotion, but my mother wouldn't let me go out in the pitch dark and cold. Buckets of water were being poured down the chimney, mixing with the soot to make a dark gravy that started to cover our tiles. When the mopping

FLAVOURS OF ROSELLO

up operation was complete I asked my grandmother why they had been panicking so much and she explained that the house had been destroyed during fighting in World War II and had then been rebuilt using the same old wooden beams rather than steel ones, so a tiny spark could have caused a great disaster by burning the whole house down.

Uncle Gesidio was well respected and admired by all the people of Pescopennataro. As the village's one-man municipal guard, he had a light green uniform, including a flat cap with a badge on the front, which he would wear when he was on patrol. His duty was to ensure that villagers did not commit any offences or cause any disturbances and that nobody committed a breach of the peace. As gamekeeper, his job was to inspect the countryside, making sure that everyone had renewed their licences and that no one went fishing or shooting out of season. Anyone who was caught would be fined on the spot, no matter who they were.

In his spare time, he would take me for walks in the countryside through large forests of oaks, elms and cedars that were planted hundreds of years ago and were now part of the village's heritage. He showed me around with great enthusiasm and pride, pointing out to me the largest trees with their long branches stretching out over our heads. The rich, thick undergrowth looked like a botanical garden, with green fern leaves, red lilies, aquilegias and wild flowers. He taught me how to appreciate the beauty of the forest and to respect the nature that he himself so very much admired.

He used to tell me how, in the winter months, the wolves, foxes and wild boars would come out of their hiding places to look for food. The village hunters would lie patiently in wait for them. The shooting of a wild boar would be a cause for special celebration. Some of the meat would be cooked in a large casserole and shared by all the hunters. The legs and shoulder would be treated and hung in the farm kitchen, where they would be smoke cured by the fire, made into ham and left to mature until the following year

One afternoon, Uncle Gesidio decided to take me to hunt wild ducks in the fields around Pescopennataro. We set out on foot and walked for several miles before we reached the small pond where these beautiful wild ducks

JULY

(*anas boscas*) were swimming. As soon as he spotted the birds, Gesidio started whispering to me to be very quiet and not to move. Suddenly he had this fantastic idea.

"Pino," he said. "Creep round behind those bushes and drive the ducks towards me." He then waited, one knee on the ground, with his double-barrelled shotgun loaded, looking up towards the sky ready to open fire. The ducks were not that stupid, however, and immediately flew in the opposite direction. When we returned home empty handed and I explained to Aunty Linda what had happened she just laughed and told Gesidio he was an idiot for expecting the ducks simply to fly over so he could shoot them. Gesidio's excuse was that it was my fault, because I had approached them from the wrong direction and they had seen me coming. And yet it was he who had told me where to walk!

The taste of ice-cream (*il gelato*) always takes me back to my childhood in Rosello. During the hot summer days and long evenings, ice cream was a real treat. I would go home to my mother and ask for some money - rarely refused! - and then return in a hurry to the piazza and Carluccio's bar. Carluccio was a very kind person, always playful and teasing. The bar, at the top end of the piazza, had two rooms, one in the front and one at the back, both very dark inside. A small light bulb hanging from the ceiling gave barely enough light to see Carluccio's face. He would wipe the top of the bar counter in rotating movements with a damp cloth every few minutes. It was almost an obsession with him to keep the counter clean.

We children were allowed only into the front part of the bar, where the shelves were sparsely stacked with a few bottles of vermouth and brandy, boxes of chocolates and sweets. A big ice-cream freezer stood just inside the door. Only adults could sit in the back bar. They did not want to be disturbed in their drinking, card playing and talking, but we would still try to poke our heads inquisitively round the side of the door to see what was going on. Carluccio's wife Lucia, would stand there, her clenched fists resting on her hips, and as soon as a few children gathered she would yell at us to get out!

On the wall either side of the front door were two colourful and well-

FLAVOURS OF ROSELLO

illustrated posters listing the different kinds of ice creams and their prices. On the left was the list of the ice-cream we could all afford, while on the right were the more expensive and mouth-watering cold desserts such as Torta al Cioccolato, Bombe Gelato, Tartufo or Cassata. When, just for a joke, we asked for the most expensive ones, Carluccio always used to insist that they were not in stock. "They are on their way," he'd say with a smile. "They will be here soon." I knew them only from the pictures on his poster.

The white-enamelled ice-cream freezer was filled up to the top with delicious ice cream, but only Carluccio was allowed to open it. He would serve you and then quickly shut the heavy lid, pressing it down hard with the palm of his hands to seal it like a tin of paint. Gesticulating as only an Italian can, with his hand in the air, he would say: "You see! It's too warm, and the ice-cream will melt quickly!"

We would walk back out into the intense heat of the deserted piazza to eat our ices, sitting around the beautiful old carved stone fountain that was shaped like a cup with cascading water over the rim. The fountain was always the main focal point in the life and soul of a village piazza. During the day, only the children would be there,while the adults would either be working in the fields or enjoying a siesta - what we call in Italy *un pisolino.*

In the heat of the afternoon, women would be sitting on their polished front door steps, whispering and chatting and enjoying the tranquillity in the shade of a balcony. In the piazza, we would sit on the curved hard cement benches around the fountain, the light breeze from the cascading water cooling our faces while we enjoyed the ice cream under the shade of the lime trees. I can still remember how delicious it tasted.

I could read on the paper cups and wrappers that it was produced in Milan and I was intrigued as to how exactly it was made and brought to Carluccio's bar. I didn't learn what ingredients were used until I was working at the Belgian Embassy in Rome, where the chef used to make fresh ice cream of every kind - Bombe, Coffee Parfait, Souffle and Sorbets. I was fascinated to see the meticulous care with which the chef prepared and presented them.

The kitchen, saucepans and other utensils all had to be thoroughly cleaned, and the beating of the eggs and sugar was all done by hand as we did not have an electric beater in those days. The creamed egg base would be left in a bowl overnight to chill properly and to improve the flavour.

The sorbets would be turned out on the same day as they were made. The special sorbetiere machine first had to be prepared. The outside was made of wood and shaped like a bucket. Inside it had an electric motor to turn the blades and an insulation chamber around the bowl where ice cubes and salt grains were added to reduce the temperature to below freezing.

A few years ago, while I was in Rome, my brother Mario, took me to visit a Bar Gelateria run by a friend of his, Cesare, and his wife, Cornelia. The freezer cabinet contained the most fantastic display of types and flavours of ice cream that I have ever seen, all of which were produced in the small kitchen at the back of the shop. They were then sold either to take away or to be eaten at tables outside the bar. As we sat there and sampled some of their specialities, my mind went back to those long, hot summer afternoons in Rosello.

FLAVOURS OF ROSELLO

INSALATA DI ASPARAGI CON PROSCIUTTO DI PARMA
ASPARAGUS SALAD WITH PARMA HAM

This is a light and delicious antipasto for the warm summer days.

2 fresh bunches of asparagus
2 fresh bunches of watercress, washed
3 eating apples
12 very thin slices of Parma ham

Sauce Vinaigrette:
4 tbsp olive oil
1 tbsp wine vinegar
1 tbsp lemon juice
2 tbsp natural yoghurt
1 good pinch mixed herbs
Salt and freshly ground black pepper

Trim and tie the asparagus. Boil in plenty of water with a little salt and 2 slices of lemon. Cook until tender to the touch but not overcooked. Lift the bunches out and plunge in cold water to stop further cooking and then drain them. Cut the asparagus stems if they are too long. Keep to one side.

To make the vinaigrette: Whisk all the ingredients together in a bowl until well combined.

Place the watercress on 6 plates or in a large serving dish, cut the apples into thin wedges and arrange them around the plate. Then beautifully and artistically arrange the Parma ham and the asparagus. Spoon the vinaigrette over the salad and serve with warm ciabatta bread.

Serves: 6
Preparation: 30 minutes

JULY

SPEZZATINO DI POLLO AL DROGONGELLO
CHICKEN FRICASSÉE WITH TARRAGON SAUCE

This is a tasty meal that you could prepare quickly while you are enjoying your friends' company.

2 tender fresh chickens, about 1.3kg/3 lbs each ,cut into pieces
Seasoned flour to coat chicken
125g / 4 oz butter
8 tbsp olive oil
6 sprigs of fresh tarragon
200ml / 6 fl oz white wine
500ml / 16 fl oz chicken stock
300ml / 9 fl oz double cream
Salt and freshly ground black pepper
2 tbsp tarragon leaves, very finely chopped

Coat the chicken pieces with the seasoned flour. In a large pan melt the butter with the oil until it is a hazelnut colour. Add the chicken pieces and brown lightly over low heat.

Add the tarragon and white wine, and then boil the liquid for about 5 minutes. Add the chicken stock. Season with salt and pepper. Cover and cook gently, turning the chicken pieces once or twice. When they are cooked lift the pieces out and arrange in an ovenproof dish. Cover with foil and keep warm. Add the cream to the sauce in the pan and reduce on low heat until the sauce becomes smooth and will coat the back of a spoon. Sieve the sauce into a saucepan and pour over the chicken. Sprinkle with more tarragon and serve.

Serves: 6-8
Preparation: 15 minutes
Cooking: 30-35 minutes

FLAVOURS OF ROSELLO

MELANZANE DI PROVINCIA
AUBERGINES A LA PROVENÇALE

This lovely aubergine dish can be served hot or cold, by itself or with a fricassée of chicken, roast veal or pork.

3 large aubergines
Coarse salt
500g / 1lb 2 oz tomatoes
1 medium onion, finely chopped
3-4 cloves of garlic, pressed
Olive oil
Salt and freshly ground black pepper
2 tbsp parsley, finely chopped

Remove the green stalks from the aubergines. Cut the unpeeled aubergines in half crossways, and cut into slices $1/2$ cm/ $1/4$ inch thick. Put on a board and sprinkle with coarse salt to draw out the moisture, leaving them for about 30 minutes to drain. Rinse in cold water and squeeze the water out gently. Pour some olive oil on a baking tray, lay the aubergines on it, overlapping each other and bake for about 20 minutes or until tender to the touch. While the aubergines are cooking, poach the tomatoes in boiling water for 1-2 minutes, skin them, cut into quarters and deseed them. Fry the onion and garlic in olive oil on a low heat until soft, then add the tomatoes and sauté quickly, ensuring that the pulp does not brown. Season and set aside.

Arrange the aubergines in an earthenware oven dish, overlapping them and pour over the tomato mixture to cover them. Return to the oven for another 25-30 minutes to finish the cooking. Sprinkle with the chopped parsley.
Serves: 6 or more
Preparation: 30 minutes
Cooking: 50-55 minutes
Oven: 180°C/350°F/Gas 4

JULY

GELATO DI TORRONE E MIELE CON SALSA DI LAMPONI
ICE-CREAM WITH HONEY AND NOUGAT WITH RASPBERRY SAUCE

This recipe was given to me by Baroness von Zuylan for whom I cooked in London.

10 egg yolks eggs size 4
200g / 7 oz sugar
2 tbsp water
6 tbsp good honey
200g / 7 oz chopped nougat
500ml / 16 fl oz double cream, lightly whipped
5 beaten egg whites
Raspberry sauce (see page 102)

Put the egg yolks, sugar and water into a large bowl over a pan of hot water, or on top of a double boiler and beat the mixture over the hot, but not boiling, water until the eggs have doubled and are a pale straw colour.

Draw off the heat, add the chopped nougat and honey and mix well. Ensure that the mixture is completely cold before adding the lightly whipped cream and the beaten egg whites (not too stiff). Fold all the ingredients together very gently and pour into a soufflé dish. Place in the freezer, stirring occasionally as the nougat may set at the base of the soufflé dish. Leave for several hours or overnight.

Serve with raspberry sauce.

Serves: 6 or more
Preparation: 10 minutes
Beating and finishing: 45 minutes
Chef's note: If the honey is too thick, place it in a bain-marié to soften it and it will be easier to fold into the mixture. The cream must be added to the egg mixture when completely cold, or it will curdle.

FLAVOURS OF ROSELLO

SALSA DI LAMPONI
RASPBERRY SAUCE

450g / 1lb fresh or frozen puréed raspberries
150g / 5 oz icing sugar
2 tbsp Kirsch (optional)
Juice of half a lemon

Put the raspberries and icing sugar into a liquidiser. Purée and sieve, add the lemon juice and Kirsch. If you prefer a sharper sauce, add more lemon juice.

This colourful sauce has a refreshing and tangy taste and accompanies many sweets. It is especially good with rich desserts, where it will be a refreshing contrast of flavours.

Makes: 450g / 1pint
Preparation: 15 minutes

AUGUST

A l'amico offre pesche e fichi
Offer figs and peaches to a friend

By August, the wheat would have been fully harvested. The men in the fields would cut the wheat with a sharp, pointed sickle, gathering it up with their free hand and laying it down in the field. Almost in the same movement they would then pull up another handful of wheat by the roots and shake off the earth before slipping it under each sheaf of wheat to tie it together, deftly pulling and twisting the ends with expert hands. The sheaves would be neatly piled together and dotted around the fields to be collected later, each farmer returning with his mare or mule and loading them onto his cart.

Tractors and any other forms of motorised farm machinery were virtually non-existent in those days so this could be a slow process, involving several journeys and often lasting all day long, from dawn 'til dusk. The sheaves would be transported to one of the fields nearer the village, where they would be built into a stack, a job that looked simple but actually required a lot of expertise. The sheaves would be laid with the straw ends to the outside to form square, outer walls and then others would be piled into the centre. Long wooden staves would then be inserted to hold them in place and these structures would be topped off with a thatched roof. From a distance they looked just like miniature houses.

For the village children, the most exciting moment was the arrival of the threshing machine. This would be pulled by a huge, bright red tractor, with smelly black smoke pouring from the exhaust pipe and two gigantic rear wheels that were wider and taller than we were. Following behind would be a gang of eight or nine men, all of them dressed in black trousers and open sandals. They would have walked miles in the hot sun to reach our village and would already be looking tired, sweaty and thirsty by the time they got to us. We used to keep a watch out, straining our eyes to be the first to spot them coming. We would run out to meet them and then follow them in, watching as they set up the machinery, ready to start threshing first thing the next morning.

The threshing machine was a square box of a contraption that looked a bit like a large garden shed on wheels. It was connected to the tractor's drive wheel by a long canvas belt and as soon as the tractor started up it would bring this red box to life. We would watch spellbound as the various interlinked belts, wheels, sieves and drawers began shaking, rattling and banging in noisy syncopation. A male worker, wearing glass goggles to protect his eyes, would pick up the sheaves with a long, thin pitchfork. He would heave them up to the top of the thresher where another man would cut the twisted straws and feed them into the machine. At the other end of the machine, a stream of shiny, sieved grains would be spewed into sacks that would quickly be filled and then taken away to be weighed (so the cost of the threshing could be fixed) before being loaded onto carts to be carried home. All this required a huge amount of hard, physical labour.

Even so, these threshing days were joyful, social occasions, almost like a festival. Whole families would turn out, including men, women and children. We would break off at midday to eat savoury tomato flan (*crostata di pomodori*) and drink wine, sitting on the grass next to our own stacks and singing local folk songs together.

AUGUST

Amid this busy scene, we children would play hide and seek and run around between sacks, enjoying all the confusion. At the end of the process, the clean straw would be pressed together into bales and piled up. The deafening clatter of the running engine and the swirling dust never ceased in the fierce heat of the August sun, known as *sol leone*, but everybody would be in a good mood. And happiest of all would be the farmers, especially if the harvest had been a good one. For them, it was the welcome reward for a long, hard year full of uncertainty and the joy and relief would show on their smiling faces.

August is when Italians like to take their holidays and even for those who could not afford to take much time off there was the national holiday of *Ferragosto*. The name *Ferragosto*, derives from the Latin, Feriae Augustae, a festival declared in honour of the emperor Augustus. Traditionally this used to be on the first day of the month named after him. Nowadays the *Ferragosto* is celebrated on the 15th August. It is a day when everybody gets a chance to rest and forget about work, to eat, drink and have a good time with family and friends.

Many people choose to get out of the towns and cities and travel to the coast, to sample the festive and regional dishes. In our village, we would mostly organise ourselves into various groups, depending on age. I always chose to join my young friends for a day in the countryside. There would usually be about forty of us, a very mixed bunch, and we would set off to enjoy a feast in the woods.

This was something on a much grander scale than just a picnic. Like a small army on the move, we took with us everything needed for a full-scale meal, including an iron cauldron - complete with a lid and a tripod from which to suspend it over the fire - kitchen utensils, plates, cutlery and glasses. There would be vast quantities of pasta, Parmesan cheese and all the ingredients necessary for pasta sauce, lamb cutlets, vegetables, tomatoes and lettuce, not to mention many cases of wine and beers. I can't remember ever bothering to take any water!

We would all meet up at seven o'clock in the piazza, amid much noisy laughter and joking, and would then set off on foot, weighed down with all our equipment and food, stumbling through uneven fields until we reached a convenient woodland spot on the banks of the river Turcano that ran down the valley. Melons, tomatoes, lettuces and beers would be placed in the fast-running water to stay cool. We would settle down for a few minutes to get our breath back before dividing up into small groups with responsibility for various tasks. Some would go off to collect wood for the fire, while others would start preparing the food. One lot would be in charge of cooking the pasta penne in the big cauldron, others would concentrate on barbecuing the lamb over hot charcoal. The entire meal (*penne Montebello*) was cooked on the spot and enjoyed al fresco in a spirit of fun and good humour. I look back on those days with great nostalgia as some of the best of my life.

Towards the end of the month, the first peaches would be sold on our village street corners. As soon as the fruit began to ripen, Luigino, the greengrocer, would come to sell his produce, which he carried in old wicker baskets on the sides of his donkey. The baskets would be filled up to the top with fresh peaches, long pointed green leaves mixed in with the fruit to set off the beautiful delicate colours of the peaches themselves. They would usually be eaten fresh, the velvety skin having been wiped clean with a cloth or simply with the palm of one's hand.

Alternatively, the fruit can be peeled, cut into segments and marinated in a good wine, either red or white. My father loves the peaches eaten this way, and it has become a ritual for him at every meal. They are supposed to be especially good for you eaten this way, but I am sure that it is '*gusto*' rather than health that accounts for the popularity of this method! The favourite recipe in our family is for peaches filled with almonds (*pesche ripiene*) and served with raspberry sauce. Irresistible!

AUGUST

CROSTATA DI POMODORI
SAVOURY TOMATO TART

A light and a delicious savoury tomato tart. Serve as a starter or as a main course with fresh salads.

For the shortcrust pastry
(Make in advance and leave to rest in the fridge)

125g / 4 oz strong plain flour
125g / 4 oz self-rising flour
125g / 4 oz butter
A good pinch of salt
1 egg yolk
4-6 tbsp cold water

For the filling:
3 eggs size 4
100ml / 3 fl oz double cream
30g / 1oz melted butter
1 tbsp fresh chopped chives
100g / 3½ oz grated Emmenthal or Cheddar cheese
Salt and freshly ground black pepper
900g / 2 lb ripe tomatoes, peeled, deseeded and cut into quarters

Pastry: Sift the flour into a bowl, and then add the salt, and the butter cut into pieces. Using one hand, work lightly until the mixture becomes "sandy" in texture. Pour in the liquids and work the mixture lightly together by hand until it forms a compact mass that will not separated. Roll into a ball wrap it in a cloth or cling-film and leave to stand for 1 hour in the fridge.

With a pastry brush, grease the inside of the tart tin and dust with a little flour. Roll out the pastry to about ½cm/ ¼inch   thick   and   line   the

25¹/₂cm/10 inch loose-based tin, ensuring that the pastry is even. Trim off any surplus and press the edges of the flan dish with your fingers to raise the pastry a little higher than the edge. Prick the pastry and place a piece of greaseproof paper over the flan, fill it with some dried beans or rice and bake blind for 15 minutes.

Preparation: 15 minutes plus resting time
Cooking: 15 minutes.
Oven: 170°C/325°F/Gas 3

Filling:

Plunge the tomatoes in boiling water for a few seconds, lift them out and then into cold water to skin them.

Arrange the cheese and the tomatoes in the base of the flan case. Beat the eggs in a bowl until light, as for an omelette. Add the cream, melted butter, chopped chives and salt and pepper. Mix well, then pour into the flan, but do not overfill. Put into a preheated oven and bake. The surface should be risen and golden.

Serves 6 or more
Preparation: 20 minutes
Cooking 23-30 minutes
Oven: 190°C/375°F/Gas 5

Chef's note: This flan is best served hot straight from the oven.

AUGUST

PENNE MONTEBELLO

600g / 1 lb 5 oz penne or spaghetti
For the sauce:
4 tbsp olive oil
1 medium onion, chopped
1 clove garlic, crushed
60g / 2 oz streaky bacon cut into small strips
100ml / 3 fl oz white wine (optional)
1 tbsp tomato puree
400g / 14 oz tin peeled tomatoes, chopped
$1/2$ tsp salt and freshly ground black pepper
2 sprigs fresh rosemary
60g / 2 oz tiny petit pois (fresh or frozen)
2 tbsp fresh chopped parsley to sprinke on top
Parmesan cheese.

Heat the oil in a saucepan and add the chopped onion, garlic and bacon. Fry on a moderate heat until the onion becomes transparent. Add the wine and reduce for 5 minutes. Add the tomato puree, peeled tomatoes, salt, pepper and rosemary. Bring to the boil. Cook on moderate heat for 20 minutes, stirring to prevent sticking. Add the drained peas and cook for another 10 minutes. Set aside.

While the sauce is cooking, fill a large saucepan with plenty of water, adding a little salt and a few drops of olive oil. Bring to the boil and cook the penne according to instructions. Before draining, add 1 cup of cold water to prevent further cooking, stir and strain. Put penne back into saucepan, add a little of the sauce, mix well and divide onto plates. Spoon remaining sauce over the top adding chopped parsley. Serve with Parmesan cheese.

Serves: 6
Preparation: 20 minutes
Cooking: 45 minutes

FLAVOURS OF ROSELLO

CROSTATA DI FICHI
FIG TART

This is a delicious way to serve figs as a dessert. Its taste and contrasting flavour with the almonds is perfect to impress your friends for a dinner party. Use can substitute the figs with plums, nectarines or pears if you prefer.

Sweet shortcrust pastry (see page 141)

For the filling:
14 fresh figs, large and firm, but not too ripe
1 litre / 2 pints cold water
100g / 3$^{1}/_{2}$ oz caster sugar
100ml / 3 fl oz white wine
1-2 strips of lemon zest

Almond cream:
125g / 4 oz icing sugar
125g / 4 oz ground almonds
125g / 4 oz unsalted butter melted
1 tbsp plain flour
2 eggs, size 4 lightly beaten

To glaze:
180g / 6 oz apricot jam
1-2 tbsp fig syrup (see method)

Make the shortcrust pastry in advance and leave to rest in the fridge.

In a saucepan combine the water, sugar, wine and lemon zest, bring to the boil and simmer for 3 minutes.

Wash the figs and make a small incision with a knife at the end of each fruit to prevent them bursting while cooking. Poach the figs in the syrup you have

110

AUGUST

made, boiling very gently for about 5 minutes or until just tender. Remove from heat and leave to cool.

With a pastry brush, grease the inside of the tart tin and dust with a little flour. Roll out the pastry to about ½cm / ¼in thick and line a 23cm / 9 in loose-based tin, ensuring that the pastry is even. Trim off any surplus and press the edges of the flan dish with your fingers to raise the pastry a little higher than the edge. Prick the pastry and place a piece of greaseproof paper over the flan, fill it with some dried beans or rice and bake blind for about 15 minutes. Leave to cool.

Melt the butter for the almond cream on a low heat in a small saucepan and leave to cool. In a bowl combine the butter with sugar, ground almonds, flour and eggs. Mix well and spread over the flan base. Lift the figs out of the syrup, drain the excess liquid and arrange them artistically over the almond cream and bake.

When cold, melt the apricot jam with the fig syrup, sieve and glaze the flan with a small brush.

Present the tart whole, cut into wedges and serve with a light sugared whipped cream.

Serves: 6 or more
Preparation: 30 minutes
Cooking: 25-30 minutes
Oven: 170°C/325°F/Gas 3 to bake the pastry,
then 180°C/350°F/Gas 4 for the filling.

FLAVOURS OF ROSELLO

PESCHE RIFIENE CON SALSA DI LAMPONI
PEACHES WITH ALMONDS AND RASPBERRY SAUCE

This is a beautiful way to serve fresh peaches and raspberries in the summer. It is another favourite of Princess Michael of Kent.

6 medium fresh ripened peaches
4 sponge finger biscuits or Savoyards made into crumbs
80g / 2 $^1/_2$ oz caster sugar
60g / 2 oz ground almonds
1 glass white wine
Raspberry sauce (see page 102)

Cut the peaches in half. Remove the stones and enlarge the centre slightly, taking care not to damage the skin. Finely chop the peach flesh. Put into a small bowl and add the almonds, the biscuits and 50g / 1 $^1/_2$ oz of the sugar. Stir the mixture well until it is like a sticky paste. Using a teaspoon divide the mixture into twelve portions, wet the palms of your hands and roll into balls. Place the balls in the centre of the peach halves and press down lightly. Grease an ovenproof dish with a little butter, sprinkle with the rest of the sugar, and pour the wine into the dish. Bake in the oven.

Remove and leave to cool. Glaze with a few spoons of warm apricot jam to give a nicer finish.

To serve: Spoon the raspberry sauce over six plates, place the halved peaches on the plates and decorate with mint leaves. Alternatively, serve on a large dish with the sauce on the side.

Serves: 6
Preparation: 20 minutes
Cooking: 20 minutes
Oven: 180°C/350°F/Gas 4

SEPTEMBER

La banda suona le prime note verso la gente e la festa comincia
The brass band blasted out its first notes to the crowds, and the
fiesta began

The end of August and the beginning of September marks the start of the tomato (*pomodori*) season. For Italians, tomatoes are the quintessential store cupboard ingredient and at this time of year everyone, all over the country, will be busy preserving fresh, plump tomatoes in bottles and jars. It is an annual rite, religiously repeated.

Huge, bright red lorries that had come all the way up from the Neapolitan area would suddenly appear on every street corner in our village. Having negotiated the narrow, winding mountain roads leading to Rosello, the drivers would hoot their horns, or cry out *"Pomodori, Pomodori"* to attract everyone's attention. Their trucks would be filled with cases and cases of beautiful, shiny red tomatoes of the San Marzano variety.

A small crowd of people would quickly gather around at the back of the lorry. The women would come out of their houses to compare the quality and price before eventually buying hundreds of kilos at a time. Saving a few lire meant a lot. "How much do they cost by the *quintale* (100kg)?" a woman might ask. "Ten thousand lire," the seller would reply. "Too dear," the woman would say, wrinkling her nose. And then the bargaining would begin. Buying in large amounts of 100 kilograms was the best way of negotiating a good price, and haggling between the vendor and the buyer was very much a part of the ritual. Eventually, a smile on the woman's face would indicate a good deal but afterwards she and her neighbours would argue fiercely over who had got the best bargain.

Tomato sauce has become one of Italy's best-known specialities. It is used on a daily basis in most Italian homes, not just on spaghetti and most other types of pasta but in many other classic Italian dishes. Canned San Marzano, the plum tomatoes with the elongated shape, are exported to the four corners of the world and are renowned for their juiciness and sweetness.

The Neopolitans claim to make the best tomato sauce in the world, *Salsa Napoletana*. The vast and fertile land in the south of Italy is blessed with a hot climate and warm sunshine for most of the year and that helps the *pomodori* to grow and ripen. They are picked by hand at exactly the right moment to obtain the very best possible freshness, smell and taste.

Tomatoes have a natural affinity with many culinary herbs, basil and oregano, especially, but also fresh parsley and marjoram. Plum tomatoes are also convenient for slicing and serving as a starter with mozzarella (*caprese*). And a simple tomato sauce can be used in many ways, with fresh clams, tuna, fish soup or sweet basil leaves added to give subtle differences in flavour.

In my childhood, home-bottled tomatoes were a winter necessity for every family. The laborious and backbreaking task of bottling the tomatoes we had bought would take almost a whole day and I used to help my mother and grandmother from an early age. It was my duty to give a hand because, as my father used to keep telling me: "At the end of the day, you are going to eat the tomato sauce as well!"

All our old bottles were kept and constantly re-used. I don't think anyone ever threw an empty bottle away. The bottles had to be washed one by one, rinsed and left to drain until the inside was dry. Meanwhile, a big cauldron of water was suspended over a huge log fire and brought to the boil. The

SEPTEMBER

tomatoes, having been carefully washed, were then poached very quickly before being lifted out and left to cool in cold water.

For the next stage, they would be put into a drum with a handle on the side that operated a bit like a butter churn, removing the skins to leave you with just the tomato pulp. This would be collected in a basin at which point a little salt would be added before it was put into the bottles. With the help of a funnel, one or two leaves of sweet basil would be pushed through the bottlenecks and some olive oil would also be poured in before the bottles were corked and tied with string.

Wrapped in tea towels, they would then be placed in a large cauldron with a layer of stones in the bottom and water would be added, brought to the boil and left to simmer for about an hour. The purpose of the stones was to absorb some of the heat and stop the bottles from heating up too quickly and exploding. Even so, there would inevitably be a few casualties, but the tea towels prevented the broken glass from flying around. When completely cold, the bottles would be removed and stored in rows in the larder or cellar, as if they were bottles of vintage wine. In our house, we used to end up with about two hundred bottles, which we would soon start to get through at a rate of nearly one-a-day.

September 7th, 8th and 9th were the three most important dates in Rosello's annual calendar. Observing a tradition that went back many centuries, this was when the village celebrated a religious feast in honour of St. Nicholas, St. Bartholomew and the Madonna of the Grace. Everybody connected with the village, even those who had moved abroad, would put their hearts and souls into these celebrations, donating money to ensure that the three days would be a great success.

A special committee organised this major event, which involved a great deal of hard work and preparation. Excitement mounted in the months beforehand as the bandstand, lights, fireworks and all the other aspects of the festivities were prepared. A member of the committee would visit every household to ask the head of the family if he would take in a musician for the three days and provide his meals. Much to our disappointment, we were never able to have a musician in our house because my father was always away at sea and we children were considered too young to keep him company at the table.

Nevertheless, we would celebrate the feast with some of our favourite dishes, including penne in tomato with mozzarella and aubergines (*penna al pomodoro e mozzarella*) and roast leg of lamb with mint and vegetables (*agnello al forno*). Being well dressed was a very important part of the occasion and along with my brothers and sisters I would try on my best outfit to make sure it still fitted, rather hoping that it wouldn't so that I could have something new.

On the morning of September 6th, the bandstand and the lights would arrive and the men would work all day to assemble them. Long wooden poles were placed in a circle with twelve panels around the side to form the basic shape of the bandstand, while a series of arches connected the poles. Inside the circle, a raised wooden floor was fixed into place and above the entrance was the proud owner's name, Adriano e Figlio, along with his logo, a collection of musical trophies. Around the top of the bandstand portraits of great composer's were hand-painted onto the wooden panels with their names written below - Verdi, Puccini, Rossini, Wagner, Bizet, Strauss and so on.

The last and most important part of the assembly was the placing in position of the big cupola, painted a beautiful dark blue to contrast with the azure sky. At the very top of the cupola, a miniature harp symbolised the music that was to be played while hundreds of tiny lights were strung around the edge. The village children would gather to watch in fascination as this gigantic jigsaw puzzle was put together.

On the opening day of the feast, the whole village would be awoken at seven o'clock by a loud volley of shots. The vibrations were so strong that the glass panels in the windows shook! I would jump out of bed and hurry to the piazza with my friends to watch the band arriving. Looking down the village road, we waited patiently for the coach to appear, our eyes fixed in one position. The grown-ups would tell us: "Put your ear to the ground and if you can hear the vibration of the wheels it means that the coach is on its way." And, of course, we would believe them!

When the musicians finally arrived, they would line up in their smart white uniforms and strike up a tune to signal the formal start of the celebrations. They would then march around the village, while committee members handed out a little picture of our patron saint to every home, collecting money as they went. All the children followed excitedly behind the band, imitating their actions. At midday, Don Peppe would say Mass and the procession would wind through the village streets, with the statue of Saint Nicholas, our patron saint, carried high on the men's shoulders.

They would always be very smartly dressed, steady on their feet and looking very serious (as if trying to say: "We are carrying a saint, it is no joke!"), while the sweat dripped down their foreheads in the heat. The ladies,

FLAVOURS OF ROSELLO

with their rosary beads in their hands, sang religious songs and prayed, while the band, with their shiny brass instruments, played on. Despite all the celebrations it was a time of peace and reflection.

The most important day of the feast is in honour of Madonna of the Grace. In a small 13th century chapel that stands on a hilltop about a mile away from the village, the image of the Virgin stands above an altar in a beautiful marble frame. This pretty chapel figures dramatically in Rosello's history since it was here, during the Second World War, that many of the villagers, including my mother and grandmother, sought refuge from German occupation forces. My mother, who had been very young at the time, told me stories of the horror and shock she went through during the days they spent crammed together in the chapel, after the Germans had forced everybody out of their homes. Since then, the chapel has become a shrine where people go to say a prayer and to light a candle.

On the day of the Madonna, the image from the chapel - a copy of which I always carry in my wallet - would be paraded around the streets of the village by a procession of women. Then, in the evening, people from nearby villages would come to join us for the festivities. The band would play famous opera arias in the fully illuminated bandstand, supplying a delightful accompaniment as people strolled past the stalls that had been set up along one side of the piazza, enjoying the cool, light breeze of the mountain air. At the same time, we youngsters played amongst ourselves, running around all over the place, buying toys, balloons, plastic trumpets and little drums to play with. A carousel went round and round, the small coloured seats full of children squealing with excitement while others queued, waiting impatiently for their turn. For us, the festival was the biggest treat of the year, providing the most joyful days of our young lives.

At around midnight on the last day, the band would finish playing and Gennarino, the man in charge of the fireworks, would wait in the darkness for the signal to begin the display. A musician with a trumpet would blast a few notes and Gennarino would ignite the first rocket, followed by an endless succession of brilliantly coloured Roman candles, cascades and Catherine

SEPTEMBER

wheels. Finally, the loudest bang of them all would signal the end of the three days of annual celebration that provided me with some of my most vivid childhood memories.

Everybody was brought down to earth later in the month when the time came to pick the potatoes. My uncle Pascquale and aunt Vincenza had a field on the hillside just outside the village and I would go to help them with the picking. As they dug up the potatoes, it would be my job to collect them. We would go on, steadily filling the sacks until the Town Hall clock struck midday. This would be the signal for us to stop work and find a patch of shade on the edge of the field, away from the hot sun. My aunt would spread out a white tablecloth and we would enjoy a picnic lunch while enjoying views of the surrounding countryside. A favourite dish was chicken with potato (*pollo con patate*). After a short break we would continue working until just before sunset.

The long summer holidays would now be coming to and end and those carefree days were over once again. I was glad enough by now, however, to return to school, to a new class and with a new companion to sit next to for the coming year.

FLAVOURS OF ROSELLO

PENNE AL POMODORO E MOZZARELLA
PENNE WITH TOMATO AND MOZZARELLA

This is a delicious and tasty vegetarian dish.

2 medium aubergines prepared and cut into 1 cm / ¹/₂in. chuncks
2 cloves garlic, peeled
100ml / 4 fl oz olive oil
300g / 10 oz fresh tomato pulp (tomatoes peeled, seeded and crushed)
500g / 1lb 2 oz penne
1 fresh mozzarella, thinly sliced
A few Parmesan shavings
Salt and freshly ground black pepper

In a fairly large frying pan, heat the olive oil with the garlic. Sauté the aubergine over a high heat until browned. Shake the pan rather than stir so the vegetable stays firm and holds its shape. When crisp, mix in the tomato pulp. Add salt and pepper and quickly remove from the heat. Meanwhile, fill up a large pan with salted water and cook the penne (according to instructions). Preferable not over overcook the pasta. Preheat the oven. Before draining the pasta, add 1 glass of cold water stir and strain the pasta and returning to the pan, stirring in the aubergine-tomato mixture. Grease an ovenproof dish with a little oil. Pour in the mixture and bake for 7-8 minutes. Remove the dish from the oven and cover with the mozzarella and Parmesan shavings. Continue to bake for a further 10-12 minutes until the cheese starts to melt and the top turns a golden brown. Add freshly ground black pepper and serve.

Serves: 6 or more
Preparation: 30 minutes
Cooking: 20 minutes
Oven: 200°C/400°/Gas 6

SEPTEMBER

BAVARESE DI PERE CON SALSA DI MORE
PEAR BAVAROIS WITH BLACKBERRY SAUCE

500g / 1lb 2 oz ripened pears
200g / 7 oz icing sugar
400ml / 12 fl oz double cream
20 or more sponge finger biscuits
5 leaves of gelatine, soaked in cold water or $1/2$ envelope gelatine soaked in cold water
Juice of $1/2$ lemon

Line the base of a 1 litre/2 pint round soufflé dish with greaseproof paper. Arrange the sponge fingers round the edge of the dish, using a little butter to secure them. Place in the fridge.

Choose good quality pears that are not too soft. Peel and halve them and scoop out the cores. Poach the pears lightly in light sugar syrup with 2 peels of lemon zest until they are slightly soft, but not overdone. Remove the lemon zest and cool the pears. Purée and then sieve them. Add the sugar and the lemon juice. Whip the cream lightly and set aside.

Drain the water from the gelatine; melt down, on a very low heat. Add to the fruit and stir. Fold in the whipped cream, mix gently with a whisk and wait until it thickens slightly. Fold it into the dish and leave to set for at least 4 hours or overnight

Remove from mould by dipping the dish in hot water for 30 seconds and invert over a platter or a dish. Decorate with whipped cream and serve with blackberry sauce. (page 122)

This type of bavarois can be made a day ahead as it keeps well in the fridge, and freezes well for several weeks.

Serves: 6 or more
Preparation: 30 minutes
Cooking: 10 minutes plus setting time

FLAVOURS OF ROSELLO

SALSA DI MORE
BLACKBERRY SAUCE

450g / 1 lb fresh or frozen blackberries
150g / 5 oz icing sugar
2 tbsp Kirsch (optional)
Juice of half a lemon

Put the blackberries and icing sugar into a liquidiser. Purée and sieve, and then add the lemon juice and Kirsch.
If you prefer a sharper sauce, add more lemon juice.

Chef's note: This sauce is nice served with any ice cream or cheesecake.

Makes: 450g / 1 pint
Preparation: 15 minutes

OCTOBER

Il vino e buono quando e vecchio, l'olio se e nuovo
The wine is good when it is old, the oil when it is new

Autumn is one of my favourite seasons. Here I am, sitting in my comfortable big armchair beside a crackling log fire. The Virginia creeper on the patio wall is turning red, the autumn leaves are tumbling down, the evenings are drawing in and there is a distinct nip in the air. I have stored apples in two wooden drawers, ready for some lovely warm apple crumble and custard through the winter.

This is the way I imagine my retirement days, when I finally hang up my white chef's jacket. But I must tell you that however much I picture this scene in my mind's eye, it is really quite uncharacteristic of me. I am not in the habit of sitting still for long, looking pensive and gazing into the fire. I always have things to do, my mind never stops racing. Caroline tells friends that when Pino gets up in the morning she never knows what he is going to be doing that day. She thinks it makes me sound more interesting and full of fun!

As a child, one of the things I most looked forward to at this time of year was walking with my grandmother to Villa St Maria, a small town just a few miles from Rosello, to visit the autumn market fair (*alla fiera*). Concettina and I would set off early in the morning, before the sun had fully risen from behind the mountains. Mist was all around the countryside, the fields were still wet with dew and the air was cool. Our journey took us partly by road and partly through woods and along footpaths. Concettina was a fast walker and I almost had to run to keep up with her.

Berfore too long we would see the church campanile and the red terracotta roofs appearing in the distance, deep in a valley near the River Sangro, and I would sigh with relief that at last we were almost there. Villa St Maria is a small town, built high on a hill like many others throughout Italy. As you approach, one of the first things you see is an enormous rock, with a steep, smooth face, like slate. During the fascist period the word 'DUCE' was daubed on it in very large capital letters. It means 'Leader" and was, of course, a reference to Benito Mussolini.

You could see the word from miles away and, being so young, I was mystified as to how they managed to write that word so large and yet so precisely on the rock-face. When I went back quite recently, I found that like anything else in life, the word 'DUCE' was fading away.

Although Villa St Maria is not that far from Rosello, the climate there is quite a bit warmer, because it is closer to sea level, and this allows a plentiful crop of fresh produce. As we walked down the valley, sweet-smelling herbs like thyme, sage and rosemary scented the morning air. On the south-facing slopes were row upon row of vines, heavy with ripening grapes while, in the orchards, the trees were laden with red apples, pears and green and brown figs - all my favourite fruits, just waiting to be picked! My idea of heaven would be to sit under a huge fig tree, holding a book in one hand and stretching out the other to pick this lovely, exotic soft fruit to eat, maybe with a few slices of Parma ham as an hors-d'oeuvre (*antipasto*) or as a fig flan (*torta di fighi*).

Further down the valley, olive groves filled the landscape. I still have in my mind the image of an old lady, dressed all in black, her silvery hair pulled back into a bun, her left hand holding tight to a long, thin wooden stick to support herself, looking around and inspecting the crop of olives to be harvested in November. These groves had stood there for hundreds of years,

OCTOBER

with their gnarled dark shapes leaning to one side, their roots protruding from the earth and their silver branches blowing in the soft wind.

By the time we reached the outskirts of Villa St. Maria, the morning would be bright with sunshine. An old, disused railway bridge was visible amongst the greenery, its four stone arches damaged and chipped away, its tracks going nowhere. Concettina explained to me that during the Second World War the Germans had blown it up while a local train was crossing and that all the passengers had been killed. The bridge had been left untouched ever since as a reminder of the horrors of the war.

As we got nearer to the town, we would meet other people going the same way and exchange pleasantries. Among them would be farmers, riding on well-groomed horses and mules and wearing their best corduroy suits with a crisp white shirt and a nearly knotted tie. Their weather-beaten faces were shiny red from long days spent working in the fields and they wore their chequered caps pulled well down over their foreheads, to shield their eyes from the morning sunlight. They would be carrying cockerels, chickens, ducks, geese or small piglets in wooden cages small enough to be tied with ropes onto the saddle. Everyone had a smile on their face, all excited at the prospect of what they might be buying or selling.

The market fairs of Villa St Maria were especially renowned throughout the district for livestock, fresh produce and farming equipment. People would come from all around the neighbouring district. All the shops in the streets leading to the big piazza would be open, with stalls selling everything you could think of, the stallholders shouting out their wares to attract the shoppers' attention.

The smell of freshly baked bread filled the air. Home made pastries and biscuits would be on display in large wooden trays. Crates and wooden boxes in front of the greengrocer's shop would be stacked high with fresh fruit and vegetables of every kind, all attractively laid out in a pattern of contrasting colours to make them appear irresistible. The pavement would already be garnished with discarded lettuce leaves, squashed oranges, bruised apples and crushed grapes, the usual casualties that did not make the grade. People would already be queueing up at the stall selling roast stuffed piglet with rosemary and garlic, to be eaten at lunchtime with slices of crusty bread. The butcher, Emilio, would have hung calves feet on a long silver hook outside his shop to signify: 'Veal, freshly killed!'

There was always one stall selling nothing but pure virgin olive oil. You could buy it either in bottles or decanted into your own container. There would be olives too, black, green or red, some kept in water in wooden tubs, others piled high in glazed terracotta pots, gleaming with their own juices and decorated with olive leaves. There were olives in oil, olives in herb-flavoured oil and olives in brine. You could, if you wished, buy just a very small amount, to eat there and then. The stallholder would tear off a piece of paper, shape it into a horn and fill it with olives for you to enjoy while walking round the fair.

People would be milling around in all directions, anxious not to miss anything, the passageways between stalls and shops crowded with members of the public. The goods on offer would be very carefully examined and expertly handled to test for quality and ripeness before a purchase was made.

Concettina had several friends in Villa St Maria, people that she had got to know well over the years since she had first started going to the fairs with her own mother. She would drop in at one house after another for a chat and a gossip. It meant so little to me at that age and I couldn't wait for her to finish talking so that we could wander back to look at the stalls.

By the time she was ready to return home we would have bought strings of garlic, onions and chilli peppers, which would be used to cure ham and homemade sausages, to be eaten with a traditional dish of beans and pasta soup during the cold winter days.

Autumn also heralded the start of the mushroom season (*la stagione dei funghi*). The altitude and the soil in our region made it perfect for mushrooms and everyone looked forward to going out into the woods and fields for the first picking. Your eyes would roam eagerly, searching for the beautiful round white gems appearing in the grass, wet with early morning dew. The joy and excitement of finding the first ones is an experience I'll never forget and there is certainly no comparison between the distinctive smell of the fresh wild mushroom and that of the cultivated mushroom.

An experienced picker knows that mushrooms grow at the foot of trees and in the greener grass patches near small stones and bushes in the fields. A mushroom bed never dies and will continue to produce a crop year after year as long as it is not disturbed or damaged by inexperienced pickers. The mushroom stems should always be cut with a stainless steel knife to sever the mushroom head in a clean and neat fashion from the stem roots. I was always taught from an early age to do it in this fashion so as not to damage the spore or the mushroom cup.

Many people ruin the appearance of the mushrooms they pick by piling them into bags that eventually fold up under the crushing weight of a heavy load. In my family we always followed the proper code of mushroom picking, carefully collecting them in baskets, so that when they came to the table their appearance remained appetisingly exquisite. The idea of getting up early in the morning is not that the mushrooms might have run away, but just that other people who set their alarms earlier will get there before you and pick the lot.

Sitting at tables outside the local bar, drinking wine and playing cards, the men in our village would boast to each other about their large finds. Every

FLAVOURS OF ROSELLO

year they would dispute one another's claim to have picked baskets of the finest and most perfumed mushrooms ever seen. They would exaggerate the size of the cups, demonstrating the diameter with their hands as if they were huge umbrellas. But, of course, they would never reveal where they had found them! They would insist on keeping this secret just for themselves, jealously guarding the source of this aphrodisiac palate teaser. "It is a place where nobody has been before and I am the only one who knows where it is," they would say.

My Uncle Luigi worked as a chef in various private houses around Italy over the years and if he happened to return to Rosello for a few days' holiday during the autumn he would go out with me, showing me where to find the best mushrooms in places he had discovered when he himself was a young boy. On these expeditions he would talk to me at length about his work in the kitchens of grand houses and about the great dishes of the Art Culinaire he had learnt to cook as a young chef.

Once, when we paused at the River Verde for a drink of fresh water from its spring, he pointed out to me some wild watercress growing in the shallow water, grabbed a handful and offered me a taste, explaining how it could be used in salads and for garnishes and soups. Little did I dream that one day I would be using these ideas for my own cooking.

My grandmother once told me another tale of mushroom picking. My father had come home on leave, and, as it was the mushroom season, he decided to set out on his own one morning to see what he could find. His search led him to a good crop of mushrooms. On his way back to the village he bumped into his friend, Iolando, and proudly showed him his full basket. Iolando was aghast and tried to convince my father that they were poisonous and should not be eaten. My father however, insisted that they were safe and proceeded home.

Later that day, he went with my mother and grandmother to cut down some trees on our land. Meanwhile Iolando got in touch with Isidoro, who was a forest manager and a great expert in wildlife, and sent him to our home. At my house, Isidoro asked my sister Savina to show him the

OCTOBER

mushrooms and after taking one look at them he made her throw the lot away, confirming that although they looked very similar to the edible variety, they were indeed poisonous. My father had intended to cook them for dinner that evening for the whole family, so perhaps it is better not to think of what might have happened. Fate had ensured that his friend was around at the right time!

As well as mushrooms, the autumn landscape around Rosello also featured bushes of wild roses (*rosa canina*) with their distinctive red hips, wild blackberry bushes laden with fruit and swathes of small thistles (*cardus defloratus*) with very sharp needles and purple heads. And, dotted here and there, you would come across a few isolated wild pear trees, groaning under the weight of the fruit they bore. These thorny shrub trees produced a tiny pear, less than one inch in diameter, which was impossible to eat raw because of its bitterness and acidity.

It always seemed such a pity that this attractive fruit should be left to rot on the tree. Then, one day, our neighbours Silvino and Angiolina invited us to a lunch party to celebrate the slaughter of their pig and, to my delight and surprise, they served these tiny pears, pickled in vinegar, with the antipasto (*hors-d'oeuvre*). They were quite delicious, an unforgettable experience!

Forty years later, after Caroline and I had left London for the countryside, we got to know a lovely Warwickshire farmer, Bryan Moore and his wife Janet, whose children James and Lucy were friends of our son Edilio. One day I went to visit their farm and what should I see but a beautiful, wild pear tree growing near their barn. This time the pears were slightly larger.

I couldn't resist asking if I could have a few pounds to take away with me. Janet laughed and asked: "What are you going to do with them Pino? You can't possibly eat them. They are far too hard." I told her: "You wait and see!" When I got home, I immediately boiled the pears in water to soften them before preserving them in a mixture of vinegar and spices filling several jars with these beautiful pickled pears (*pere sotto aceto*) When I gave one to Bryan and Janet they were as surprised as I had been that day when Silvino and Angiolina first introduced me to this rare delicacy.

FLAVOURS OF ROSELLO

FUNGHI DI BOSCO SU CROSTINI
WILD MUSHROOMS ON CROUTONS

1 kg / 2 lb 2 oz Porcini or Cantarelli or wild mushrooms of your choice
100 ml / 3 fl oz olive oil
60g / 2 oz butter
2 cloves garlic crushed
2 tbsp freshly chopped parsley
Salt and freshly ground black pepper
6 slices of bread
6 tbsp olive oil
30g / 1oz butter

With a pastry cutter, cut 7 ½cm/ 3 in.circles out of bread and fry them in plenty of oil and butter. Drain off the excess fat on kitchen paper and add a pinch of salt. Keep warm.

Wash the mushrooms delicately, drain and pat dry with a kitchen cloth. Detach the stems from the caps. Slice them to a medium thickness. Heat the oil and butter, add the garlic and cook till lightly brown.

Add the mushrooms and sauté on a lively heat for 4-5 minutes. Stir while cooking and season with salt and pepper. Remove the garlic and spoon the mushrooms over the croutons. Sprinkle with parsley and serve.

Serves: 6
Preparation: 30 minutes
Cooking: 5-8 minutes

OCTOBER

MANZO IN VINO ROSSO
BEEF IN AMARONE WINE

This recipe was very kindly given to me by Mr Stephen Dover, Consultant in Oral and Maxillofacial surgery, at the Queen Elizabeth Hospital in Birmimgham.who I met while staying in the hospital for my right cheek and lip reconstruction.

This is one of his favourite recipes, a beef stew cooked in an Italian wine marinade. Pronounce the name of the wine like Luciano Pavarotti would, col bel canto: Vhii-no Am-mhrroh-nay.

1 ¹/₂ kg / 3lb 6oz silverside or fillet of beef
1 carrot sliced
6 small shallots
1 small leek cut into fine strips
60ml / 2lb oz olive oil
1 bouquet garni (sprig of parsley, thyme, a bay leaf)
1 tbsp tomato pureé
1 bottle of Amarone wine
500ml / 16 fl oz beef or vegetable stock
Salt and freshly ground black pepper
Watercress to garnish

Mix in a bowl the wine, carrot, leek, shallots, bouquet garni, garlic, tomato pureé and a few rounds of black pepper. Add the beef and leave overnight in the fridge, covered with cling-film.

Remove the meat and seal on all sides, using the heated olive oil in a fairly large saucepan. Season with salt and pepper. Remove the fat, deglaze the pan with all the marinade, and add the stock. Bring to boil, season lightly, cover and place in the oven. When the meat is cooked, lift the meat out the pan and leave to stand in a warm place.

Strain the marinade and push all the vegetables through a fine sieve and add to the gravy. Thicken the sauce lightly with a little cornflour mixed with water. Adjust the seasoning. Cut the meat into slices, and lay on a shallow dish. Pour the sauce over the meat, garnish with the watercress and serve.

Serves: 6 or more
Preparation: 30 minutes
Cooking time: 2 - 2 ½ hours
Oven: 180°C/350°F/Gas Mark 4

CAROTE NOVELLE GLASSATE
GLAZED BABY CARROTS

24 baby carrots, with their ferny tops
60g / 2oz butter
A good pinch of caster sugar
6 coridander leaves washed
Salt and freshly gound black pepper

Trim the carrot tops, leaving on 2 cm /1 in of leaves. Peel and refresh carrots in cold water. In a large pan, melt the butter with a pinch of salt and the sugar. Add the carrots in a single layer and barely cover with cold water. Bring to the boil. Cover with a lid or buttered greaseproof paper and simmer gently for about 10 minutes. Remove the cover, add the coriander leaves and reduce the liquid until the carrots are glazed. Season with a few turns of black pepper. This will not only give the carrots an attractive glaze, but will also concentrate the flavour.

Serves: 6
Preparation: 10 minutes
Cooking: 10 minutes

NOVEMBER

Il giorno di San Martino, stappa la botte a si spilla il vino
On Saint Martin day, you cork the barrel and taste the wine

Early in November, with the days drawing in fast, people would start to gather together in the evenings to spend their time round the kitchen fire. Friends, neighbours and family would all be there. The adults would sit around chatting and telling stories while the children would be on the floor, helping to strip the dried leaves from the maize cobs.

The corn would have been harvested towards the end of the previous month and brought back home in large white sacks. These would be stored in the basement before being brought up into the kitchen in a large wicker basket and emptied into a pile on the floor, ready to be stripped. The leaves were pulled right back and remained attached to the end of the corn. My grandmother would make them into long raffia plaits by which the cobs would be suspended from the balcony railing to dry out in the warm November sun. When we found a good brown corn beard (the hairs at the top of the corn), we would hold it under our noses, pretending they were moustaches! As a treat, a few tender white cobs of corn were sometimes placed over the glowing embers to roast.

While all this was going on, a neighbour, sitting around the lovely warm fire, might start to recount the latest village news. With nothing much else to do, these long dark evenings provided a great opportunity for gossiping between the different families. There would be talk of young couples planning to get married in the spring and speculation about what might have happened to the many villagers who had left Rosello after the war and emigrated to South America to find a new life and to seek their fortunes. I would prick up my ears, curious to know more about all this but whenever I started asking any questions, they would answer that I should be quiet and mind my own business, that I was too young to know about such things.

Domenico Valerio, my mother's brother, also known as 'Mimi' for short, was one of those who had gone to Argentina at a very young age, seeking a better life as a builder. I was too young to remember when he left, but I remember when his wife Anita and their son Nicolino went to join him. That was a very sad day. It was the morning of the first day of the feast of September, normally such a happy time, and my entire family were numbed. My mother, I remember, was particularly upset, her eyes shiny with tears. There were kisses and goodbyes in every direction as Anita and Nicolino left for Naples, where they were to board the ship bound for Argentina. We knew that it would be a long time before we saw them again but we never imagined that it would be thirty-six years before they all came home.

We couldn't discuss or talk about the latest film on television or the cinema, as we had neither. So stripping the corn and gossiping about our neighbours was our only entertainment. As we worked, we would have a coffee and sometime a slice of apple flan (*torta di mele*) prepared by my mother. We might also sing folk songs to make the time go by more happily.

After hanging the corn out to dry we had to wait until the cobs were hard and shiny before taking them down from the balcony railings and beating them with heavy wooden sticks to separate the yellow niblets from the hard, inner cores, which we later burned as firewood. The niblets were collected and then spread out on canvas in the piazza to let them dry out even more

NOVEMBER

before they were stored away. I was always captivated by the many beautiful shades of yellow, glimmering in the autumn sun.

Each corner of the piazza would be covered in sheets of canvas, with hardly any space left for people to walk between them. Women would have marked their space with stones the evening before they laid out their corn, in order to ensure that their place was not taken by somebody else. First thing in the morning, the sacks would be emptied onto the canvas. The women would often stay there all day, guarding and raking over the yellow corn. Towards the end of the afternoon, just before sunset when the air became cooler, the old ladies, dressed in black, would sit down and sieve the corn from the chaff. The corn was then stored in sacks to be made into flour for the winter. During our recreation time at school, we children would come out and annoy the ladies by pretending to walk over the corn, or lifting up the canvas before they chased us away with an old broom.

The first two days of November are very important in the Christian calendar. November 1st is All Saints' Day, when we remember all the saints who do not have their own designated day during the year. November 2nd is All Souls' Day. This is to commemorate the dead. Every year we would visit the cemetery to place chrysanthemums and other flowers on the graves, to light a nightlight and to pray over the graves. Above all, it is a day when everybody must pay their respects to their lost ones.

The Italians maintain strong family ties and this celebration has a special and heartfelt significance for them. Here I take a leaf from Domenico D'Amato's book, a passage in which an elderly gentleman recounts the village life of an older generation: *"It has been written that the civility of a nation is reflected in the love shown for the departed one."* There is also an old Latin quote, *'maxima debetur defunctis reverentia,'* which means: "It is a principle that reverence is owed to the deceased."

All Souls Day is followed on November 11th by St Martins's Day. This, traditionally, is when Italy's wine makers open and taste the wine they have made, an opportunity for celebrations of a more light-hearted kind, with much good-natured competition to see who has produced the best vintages.

FLAVOURS OF ROSELLO

By now the days are starting to get both shorter and colder. And yet still, occasionally, you would get one of those glorious late autumn days when in a sheltered spot, the sun could still warm your bones. They were a special blessing, like a gift before the winter months were upon us. Every afternoon outside Il Palazzo, the large building in the piazza, you would see a group of elderly gentlemen sitting at the front door on stone steps that had been highly polished by their backsides!

They would soak up this mellow sunshine, enjoying a little conversation,

reminiscing, perhaps, about the past and savouring the peace and quiet of village life. Just before sunset they would slowly return home to the warmth of the kitchen, to sit beside a lovely crackling log fire with maybe a bowl of tasty dried pea soup with smoked bacon (*piselli secchi e pancetta affumicata*). They would continue to return again each afternoon until, eventually, looking towards the horizon, they would see the mist rising from the valley and dark clouds would begin to appear over the mountains.

"Is it going to snow?" one of the men, Carmine, might ask.

"Probably," would come the reply from Antonino. "There is a chill in the

NOVEMBER

air and the wind is starting to get up."

The autumn leaves, with their subtle colours of burnished gold, copper and russet, would form a thick carpet under the trees, the countryside would begin to feel silent and empty and, soon, the first snowflakes would fall to the ground. My grandmother would smile and say: "Wait till we get the white flies, wait till we get the white flies, you will see." These words used to echo in my head when I was very small. I never quite understood what she meant by the 'white flies,' so I just smiled and nodded.

Although we children welcomed the snow, it was not so much fun for the adults. It meant warm clothing had to be bought, lots of wood was needed to burn and extra provisions had to be laid by in case we got snowed in and cut off in the months ahead. Such things were of no concern to us youngsters who saw it as an opportunity for lots of fun and games.

After school we would all meet at one particular spot in the village. It was at a point where the street sloped steeply downwards and we would ski with our homemade skis, tumbling and falling down, getting soaking wet up to our knees. My grandmother would eventually come and take me home, but she would almost have to drag me away by force.

That was never the end of it though! My mother would scream and shout at me, exasperated by my bad behaviour and would hit me over the head with whatever kitchen utensil she happened to have in her hand at the time. After a little while she would calm down and I would pull my heavy shoes and socks off my feet and leave them to dry by the fireside, ready for school the next day. We went through the same routine nearly every day during the winter. I wanted to learn to ski and to be with my school friends, and when you are that age you forget to worry about getting wet and being home in good time!

FLAVOURS OF ROSELLO

CREMA DI PISELLI SECCHI E PANCETTA AFFUMICATA
DRIED PEA SOUP WITH SMOKED BACON

A perfect soup for cold wintry days.

250g / 8 oz smoked bacon, chopped
250g / 8 oz potatoes peeled and chopped
250g / 8 oz dried peas, soaked overnight in water
2.2 litres / 4 pints chicken stock
100ml / 3 fl oz double cream
4 tbsp oil
1 large chopped onion
Salt and freshly ground black pepper

Heat the oil in a fairly large saucepan; add the chopped bacon and fry until crisp. Remove from the pan and set aside.

Put the chopped onion in the pan and fry until transparent. Add the hot stock, potatoes, salt and well-rinsed peas. Boil rapidly for 10 minutes and then simmer for 1 hour 20 minutes.

When cooked, leave to cool slightly before liquidising and straining through a fine sieve.

Serve the cream soup with a swirl of double cream, and sprinkle with the crispy bacon.

Serves: 6
Preparation: 15-20 minutes
Cooking: 1½ hours

Chef's note: Vegetarians can substitute the bacon with celery and the chicken stock with a vegetable one.

NOVEMBER

QUAGLIE ARROSTE CON MELE
ROASTED QUAIL WITH APPLES

A beautiful autumn dish, and delicious for a dinner party.

6 quails, ready for cooking
3 tbsp cooking oil
100g / 4 oz butter

Sauce:
200ml / 6 fl oz red wine
500ml / 16 fl oz quail stock or chicken stock
6 medium, cooking apples peeled and cut into 6 segment pieces
2 tbsp brown sugar
1 pinch of cinnamon
Juice of half lemon
Salt and freshly ground black pepper
Watercress to garnish
6 slices white bread cut round, and fried in
60g / 2 oz butter

Beurre manié:
60g / 2 oz butter, softened and mixed with
60g / 2 oz flour

Heat the oil and half the butter in a sauté-pan and sauté the quail on low heat for about 5 minutes, turning them to ensure they are browned all over. Season with salt and pepper, place the quail in the oven and roast for about 15-20 minutes, basting half way through. Quails take about 20 to 25 minutes to cook in total, depending on their tenderness.

In a separate pan sauté the apple quarters in the remaining butter over a medium heat. Add the brown sugar, a pinch of cinnamon, and the lemon juice and turn. Once they are a golden colour take off the heat and keep warm. The apple should be soft but not mushy.

Fry the white bread in butter until golden and set aside on a kitchen paper towel. Remove the quails from the oven and keep warm.

To prepare the sauce: Skim the fat off the cooking juices. Add the wine and reduce a little over a direct heat. Add the warm chicken stock and bring to the boil. Allow to reduce a little and thicken the sauce slightly by adding the beurre manié, a little at time. Adjust seasoning and strain into a saucepan. Keep warm.

To serve: Arrange the birds on the croutons on warm plates or a large serving dish. Pour a little sauce over each one and arrange the apple around them. Decorate with watercress. Serve the remaining sauce separately.

Serves: 6
Preparation: 1 hour
Cooking: 20-25 minutes
Oven: 200°C/400°/Gas 6

NOVEMBER

CROSTATA DI MELE
APPLE FLAN

This is a simple and very popular recipe for the Crostata.

For the sweet shortcrust pastry :
125g / 4 oz plain flour
125g / 4 oz self raising flour
125g / 4 oz butter
1 egg yolk
4-6 cold water or milk
30g / 1 oz sugar
Good pinch of salt

 Sift the flour into a bowl, and add the salt, sugar and the butter cut into pieces. Using one hand, work lightly until the mixture becomes "sandy" in texture. Pour in the liquids and work the mixture lightly together by hand until it forms a compact mass that will not separate. Roll into a ball, wrap it in a cloth or cling-film and leave to stand for 1 hour in the fridge. The quantity of this pastry is ample to line up to a 25cm/10inch flan tin.

 Generally, I prefer to make the dough the day before I need it and leave it overnight in the fridge. Remember to leave it for a while at room temperature before use.

For the filling:
5 medium cooking apples about 700g / 1lb 8 oz weight
1egg yolk, size 4
1 tbsp caster sugar
1 tbsp cornflour
100ml / 3 fl oz double cream
2 tbsp brandy or rum (optional)
15g / $1/2$ oz caster sugar
200g / 7 oz good apricot jam

Make the pastry well in advance and leave to rest. Meanwhile, peel the apples, cut them in half and core them. Set aside.

With a pastry brush grease the inside of the tart tin and dust with a little flour. Roll out the pastry to about ½cm / ¼ inch thick and line the 23cm/10 inch loose-based flan tin, ensuring that the pastry is even. Trim off any surplus and press the edges of the flan dish with your fingers to raise the pastry higher than the edge. Put an apple facing down on a chopping board and with a sharp knife cut the apple thinly almost to the edge, press the apple down and away from you so that they will fan out without falling into separate slices. Arrange artistically over the pastry.

In a small bowl combine the egg yolk, sugar, and cornflour and mix well. Then add the double cream and the liqueur. Stir to a smooth paste. Pour over the sliced apples. Sprinkle with the sugar and bake. You can finish the dish off under a very hot grill to turn the apples well brown.

When completely cold, press the apples slightly down with a palette knife to level the top. Melt the apricot jam with 1-2 tablespoons of water, sieve it and brush over the flan to an even glaze.

Serves: 6 or more
Preparation 20 minutes
Cooking: 30-35 minutes
Oven: 190°C/375°F/Gas 5

DECEMBER

L'odore d'arance freshe, la fraganza e il dolce sapore
The smell of the fresh oranges, their fragrance and their sweet taste

Christmas was a most magical and unforgettable time in my childhood. Even now, I can close my eyes and picture exactly how the village and the surrounding countryside looked, covered in a white blanket of snow. Frozen icicles would form all around the stone bowl of the fountain and the crystal clear running water would gush through the shiny icicles, breaking the quietness in the piazza. A tall pine tree, freshly cut from the woods that encircled the village would be placed in the centre of the piazza, with hundreds of tiny lights to symbolise and to celebrate the Christmas season.

One entered the village food store through an old wooden door, the bottom half carved and the top half glass-panelled to let the light through. A warm glow came from a coal brazier in the middle of the shop and the rich aroma of our traditionally-baked Christmas cakes hung in the air. Hundreds of Panettone were suspended on strings all around the store. There would be nougat bars of all sorts and sizes, beautifully wrapped in shining white paper, stockings filled with the most exciting varieties of sweets and chocolates, dried figs and rows of wooden boxes filled to the top with citrus fruits wrapped up in a fine gold and orange paper.

On one wall there used to be a recess, with shelves and glass doors, where Flavio, the store owner, would display a large collection of Nativity figures, all of them beautifully hand-painted. We children would go into the shop mostly just to gaze at them in wonderment and only very occasionally to buy. I had always wanted to have the crib as the centrepiece of my own Nativity scene, but it was very expensive. I remember pleading with my grandmother Felicetta to buy it. In the end I literally dragged her into the shop and,with help from Flavio, persuaded her to pay five hundred lire for it. That was the equivalent of about thirty pence in today's money, but a fortune at that time.

There was much keen competition between the village children to see who could create the best Nativity scene. I would go out into the countryside with my friends Antonio and Lucio in search of the mosses and ivy branches we used to decorate our grottoes. We would then spend hours composing the scene with the animals, the Three Wise Men, Mary, Joseph, the baby Jesus - and, of course, the crib!

There was a tradition in Rosello, dating back many centuries, whereby the children of the village went out two or three days before Christmas Eve to collect wood for a huge bonfire. We transported the wood on our homemade sledges as best we could, using all our strength to haul it along to a site next to the piazza.

Once the bonfire had been built, an adult would take charge of the preparations for lighting it on Christmas Eve. The idea behind this tradition was that on the night baby Jesus was going to be born, the fire would keep him warm. Once it was ablaze, we would all gather around, hands outstretched to feel the warmth, watching as the flames leapt high towards the clear night sky. The younger children would run and fall in the snow, while others held lighted sparklers, making patterns by rotating their hand in the dark. Everybody would be smiling, their faces revealing joy and

DECEMBER

happiness as they exchanged the greeting: "Buon Natale, Buon Natale."

When the flames eventually died down, we would return home for what was always a fairly simple Christmas Eve supper, a light meal of spaghetti with garlic and parsley in olive oil (*aglio e prezzemolo*), followed by a traditional homemade farm cheese, like Provolone, which was eaten with home-baked bread.

On Christmas morning the house would be a hive of noisy and animated activity as we all busied ourselves dressing up in our best clothes. My mother would stay at home, preparing our lunch, while my brothers and sisters and I went out to wish all our relations a Happy Christmas, a gesture appreciated even more by us when the grown ups would put their hands into their pockets and give us some change.

Afterwards, the whole family went to church. Later, I would meet my friends outside Carluccio's Cafe in the piazza, where we counted our money and played Sbattarielle. This is a very old game, played with a handful of coins, the outcome of which is decided by whether they come up heads or tails, and those few lire you had been given could be lost straight away!

Although, traditionally in Italy, we used to get our presents at Epiphany rather than on Christmas Day, young children would still write letters to Father Christmas, as they do elsewhere, telling him a nice little story about how good they had been and how they were always obedient and never made their parents angry, in the hope that they would be rewarded with some money or a present later. In our family, these letters would be carefully placed, under the plate at the head of the table where my father usually sat on those rare occasions when he could get home on leave ready for him to read. Noticing this, he would pretend to change his seat, just for a joke.

Our kitchen would be full of festive smells and steaming pots. The table was laid with the best white tablecloth and sparkling cutlery in preparation for this important meal and the Christmas tree laden with decorations and lights.

Our traditional Christmas lunch was an antipasto, consisting of home cured ham and pickled vegetables, followed by tortelli with spinach and ricotta, (*tortelli con spinaci e ricotta*), roasts goose with apple and chestnuts (*oca con mele e castagne*) and fine sliced fried potatoes in goose fat (*patatine fritte in grasso d'oca*). This was served with a selection of winter vegetables followed by the traditional Panettone.

We would drink wine from our own Abruzzo region, Montepulciano D'Abruzzo. Children would be offered wine with water as an introduction to this grown up taste. The best part of our meal was when the Panettone was brought to the table, cut up and served with Spumante wine. This was followed by Italian nougat, walnuts, dried figs, mandarins, and oranges from Sicily and finished off with Expresso coffee and liqueurs. The feast would be spread over several hours, with lots of chatter and laughter around the table,especially if my father had been able to join us. He would always have lots of exciting news about life on board his ship. At the end of the meal we would move back into the room next door and collapse in front of a roaring fire. Outside the air was cold and the snow would turn crisp beneath a dark blue sky on clear frosty nights. I would go out to gaze at the heavens, wishing this wonderful day could last forever. As another year in the life of Rosello came to an end, I would find myself wondering what the next would bring. How amazed I would have been if you had told me then how far away from home the future was destined eventually to lead me. Now I can only look back with nostalgia to those days long gone by.

DECEMBER

SPAGHETTTATA CON AGLIO E PREZZEMOLO
SPAGHETTI WITH GARLIC AND PARSLEY

This is one of the easiest and quickest dishes of spaghetti you have ever made. It is very tasty and full of flavour. It's origins are in the humble shantytowns of Rome, but now it is a favourite amongst the city's aristocracy who enjoy spaghetti amongst friends in the late-hours of the night.

600g / 1lb 5 oz good quality fine spaghetti
12 tbsp olive oil
3 cloves garlic, peeled and very finely chopped
3 tbps chopped parsley
Salt and freshly ground black pepper

Chop the garlic and keep to one side, then do the same with the parsley. Bring a little salted water to the boil in a fairly large saucepan. Cook the spaghetti until tender but *al dente* (firm to the bite).

Meanwhile pour the olive oil into a frying pan on a very low heat. First add the garlic and fry for a very short time, bearing in mind not to brown it or it will taste bitter. Then add the chopped parsley and turn off the heat. Add to the frying pan three large ladles full of water from the pasta and keep to one side.

Take the spaghetti pan away from the heat and add one large glass of cold water. Stir, then strain and return to the pan. Add half the sauce and a few rounds of black pepper, toss and mix well.

To serve: Place the spaghetti in a large deep dish or on individual plates. Pour over the remaining sauce and serve immediately.

Serves: 6
Preparation: 15 minutes
Chef's note: It is very important to add the water from the pasta, as the spaghetti will quickly absorb the oil and become dry and glue-like.

FLAVOURS OF ROSELLO

PASSATINA CECI CON GAMBERI
CREAM OF CHICK PEA SOUP WITH PRAWNS

This is an old Italian cream soup recipe from our Abruzzi region. Although it is served much thicker in Italy as a pureee, and not sieved, I prefer to serve it smoother, to give a more refined texture.

400 / 14 oz chickpeas
12 large cooked prawns
4 litres / 8 pints cold water
4 crushed cloves of garlic
2 fresh sprigs of rosemary
1 small chopped onion
6 tbsp olive oil
Salt and freshly ground black pepper.

Soak the chickpeas in water for at least 10 hours. Drain and rinse. Cook, boiling rapidly for 10 minutes, removing foam with slotted spoon. Add 2 cloves of garlic and rosemary. Reduce the heat, cover and simmer for a further 2 hours until soft.

Fry the onion and garlic in olive oil over a low heat until softened. Process the drained chickpeas in a food mixer with half the liquid, the onion and garlic. Sieve and add more liquid to thin the mixture down - you should have at least 1 $\frac{1}{2}$ litres of cream soup. Adjust seasoning.

Peel the prawns, cut them in half lengthways and keep warm in hot water. Pour the soup into deep plates and arrange the prawns on top. Just before serving, dress the soup with a swirl of good olive oil. Serve with hot crusty garlic bread.

Serves: 6
Preparation: 30 minutes
Cooking: 2 hours

DECEMBER

PORRI BRASATI ALL'OLIO D'OLIVA
BRAISED LEEKS IN OLIVE OIL

6 Leeks medium size
4 tbsp virgin olive oil
Good pinch dried, mixed herbs
Salt and freshly ground black pepper
1 tbsp chopped parsley

Cut off the roots and green tops, and then remove the coarse outer leaves. Cut the leeks in half widthways and wash carefully in plenty of cold water. Place the leeks in a lidded saucepan big enough to accommodate them. Pour in just enough cold water to cover the bottom of the pan, usually about half a glass. Add the olive oil, mixed herbs and salt and pepper. Cover the pan and cook the leeks on a very low heat to let the flavours infuse. Serve in a warmed dish and sprinkle with fresh parsley.

Chef's note: This can be cooked ahead and transferred with its own juice into an ovenproof dish and reheated in the oven.

Serves: 6
Preparation: 5 minutes
Cooking 10-15 minutes

OCA CON MELE E CASTAGNE
GOOSE WITH APPLE AND CHESTNUTS

1 goose weighing about 3·5-4·5kg/8-10lb
60g / 2 oz butter
10 sweet apples, peeled, cored and sliced thinly
450 g/ 1 lb can chestnut pureé
1 egg size 4
quarter glass brandy (optional)
Salt and freshly ground black pepper
300g / 10 oz can chestnuts, drained weight, quartered
1 litre / 2 pints giblet stock

Clean the goose thoroughly with a damp cloth and pat dry.

Melt the butter in a frying pan and gently fry the apples with two tablespoons of sugar until they are just beginning to soften. Set one third aside and stir the rest into the chestnut purée with the egg, half the chestnuts, the brandy and the salt and pepper. Mix well, and use this to stuff the bird. Using a small spoon put a little stuffing in the neck end and the remainder in the back cavity. Truss the bird with a needle, which has an eye large enough to take a piece of string. If a trussing needle is not available, use poultry skewers and string to secure the bird. Prick the skin all over with a fork and rub with salt and pepper.

Preheat the oven and place the goose on a wire rack in a roasting pan. Roast for 45 minutes to draw off the fat, and then turn the oven down and keep on roasting, basting the bird occasionally to brown the skin. After 2 1/2 hours drain the fat and keep aside. Remove the bird and keep warm on a serving dish, allowing the bird to rest for 20 minutes before serving. Drain off the fat from the tin. Add 6 level tablespoons of flour and mix with a wooden spoon to make light gravy with the giblet stock. Adjust the seasoning and sieve the gravy.

DECEMBER

Carve the goose and serve with the remaining apples slices warmed in butter and the remaining quartered chestnuts.

Serves: 6
Preparation: 30 minutes
Cooking: 45 mins. plus 2 1/2 hours
Oven: 200°C/400°F/Gas 6 then turn down to 170°C/325°F/Gas 3

PATATINE FRITTE IN GRASSO D'OCA
SLICED POTATOES FRIED IN GOOSE FAT

700g / 1 1/2 lb white potatoes
Goose fat
Salt and freshly ground black pepper

Peel the potatoes, rinse them in cold water and slice so they are about 1/2 cm / 1/8 in. thick and cut into rings. Bring a large pan of lightly salted water to the boil and throw in the potatoes. Par-boil the sliced potatoes for 5 minutes. Preheat the oven. Drain the potatoes and shake well.

Pour enough melted goose fat into a roasting tin to cover the base of and place it in the oven. Leave to get hot. Remove from the oven and put in the potatoes, turning them so that they are well coated with the goose fat. Return into the oven and let the potatoes cook until a golden crust has formed on both sides. Add salt and pepper and turn them. Continue cooking and turning until both sides have a nice crust. After 20-25 minutes, test with a fork to see if they are cooked.

Preparation: 20 minutes
Cooking 30-35 minutes
Oven: 180°C/350°F/Gas 4

FLAVOURS OF ROSELLO

SOUFFLÉ DI CASTAGE E COGNAC
CHESTNUT SOUFFLÉ WITH BRANDY

This exquisite dessert soufflé always seems appropriate for a misty cold autumn evening to end a dinner party, and it also makes an unusual treat for the family. Ready-made chestnut purée makes this a very easy recipe to prepare.

300g / 10 oz chestnut purée, unsweetened
100ml / 3 fl oz milk
90g / 3 oz sugar
40g / 1½ oz butter
2 tbsp brandy
3 egg yolks, size 4
6 beaten egg whites
Icing sugar to dust

Butter the sides and base of a 1 litre/2 pint soufflé dish, sprinkle with caster sugar and tip out the excess.

Boil the milk, add the butter and sugar and mix in the chestnut purée well. Allow to cool. Preheat the oven.

Add the brandy and egg yolks. Beat the egg whites with a pinch of salt until it forms peaks and then fold gently with a wooden spoon into the chestnut mixture.

Pour into the soufflé dish and bake for about 40 minutes. When ready, dust with icing sugar and serve with double cream.

Serves: 6
Preparation: 30 minutes
Cooking: 40 minutes
Oven: 200°C/400°F/Gas 6

RECIPES

STARTERS

Aunty Angiolina's Tagliatelle with tomato sauce	54
Celeriac and poached eggs au gratin	37
Croissant with scrambled eggs and smoked salmon	114
Hors-d'oeuvre	30
Polenta with sausages	43
Potato dumplings	40
Snails in tomato and mint	60
Stuffed tomatoes	26
Wild mushrooms on croutons	130

SOUPS and SAUCES

Beans and Pasta soup	25
Blackberry sauce	122
Bolognese sauce	51
Cream of chick pea soup with prawns	148
Pea soup with smoked bacon	138
Pesto sauce	63
Raspberry sauce	102
Rocket sauce	89
Tomato sauce	42

SALADS and SIDES

Asparagus salad with Parma ham	98
Aubergines a la Provencale	100
Braised Leeks	149
Country vegetables	28
Fried courgette flowers	73
Glazed baby carrots	132
Potatoes fried in goose fat	151
Rosello bread	27
Summer salad	87
Tuna and bean salad	71

MAIN COURSES

Beef in Amarone wine	131
Chicken fricassee with tarragon sauce	99
Devilled Chicken	72
Easter Pie	61
Fox stew	38
Goose with apple and chestnuts	150
Papardelle with pesto sauce	62
Lamb with red wine	64
Linguini with seafood	84
Penne with tomato and mozzarella	120
Penne Montebello	109
Pork chops with gherkins	31
Roasted quail with apples	139
Saffron risotto	86
Salmon escalopes with rocket sauce	88
Smoked salmon	75
Spaghetti with garlic and parsley	147
Spaghetti with pistachios and sweet basil	74
Tomato tart	107

DESSERTS and CAKES

Apple flan	141
Cherry tart	90
Chestnut souffle with brandy	152
Chocolate and walnut cake	65
Easter waffles	52
Fig tart	110
Ice cream with honey and nougat with raspberry sauce	101
Iced Grand Marnier souffle	76
Peaches with almonds and raspberry sauce	112
Pear bavarois with blackberry sauce	121
Sweet fritters	44
Tarallo cake	50
Tiramasu	32